THE
MEDIEVAL SCENE

AN INFORMAL INTRODUCTION
TO THE MIDDLE AGES

BY

G. G. COULTON

CAMBRIDGE
AT THE UNIVERSITY PRESS 5493
1967

PUBLISHED BY
THE SYNDICS OF THE CAMBRIDGE UNIVERSITY PRESS

Bentley House, 200 Euston Road, London, N.W. 1
American Branch: 32 East 57th Street, New York, N.Y. 10022

First printed   1930
First paperback
    edition   1959
Reprinted   1960
    1961, 1964, 1965,
    1967

First printed in Great Britain at the University Press, Cambridge
Reprinted by offset-litho by Percy Lund, Humphries and Co., Ltd, Bradford

PREFACE

THE greater part of this little book, dealing with social conditions, was delivered as a series of broadcast talks in the autumn of 1929, and was published from week to week in *The Listener*. All that concerns the mind of the Middle Ages is reprinted or adapted from my article in *Harmsworth's World History* (chapter 117); and I have to thank the Editor for his kind permission to reproduce it here.

ST JOHN'S COLLEGE, CAMBRIDGE

August 1930

CONTENTS

ILLUSTRATIONS

PLATES

Between pages 54 and 55

TEXT-FIGURES

CHAPTER I

Chaos and Reconstruction

WE cannot understand the medieval mind unless we put ourselves first at the starting-point of medieval society. For convenience, let us here include the so-called Dark Ages and define the Middle Ages as the period which begins with the break-up of the Roman Empire and ends with the Reformation. No hard and fast line can be drawn at either end. To begin with, stable government still survived in some parts of Europe for many generations after the barbarian invasions had broken it down elsewhere. Again, Luther's preaching brought parts of Germany in 1517 to a more definite religious revolution than that of the so-called Reformation Parliament of England in 1530. Again, the Renaissance had begun to influence Italian thought in 1350 more than it influenced French thought in 1450 or English in 1500. The earlier half, the Dark Ages, may be reckoned from 400 to 1000; the next five centuries form the Middle Ages in a more special sense, *le haut moyen âge*, as French historians call it.

Here we must treat the two continuously, as, of course, they were continuous; and if, for brevity's sake, we must often generalise epigrammatically, therefore it must be borne steadily in mind that no unqualified distinction between medieval thought on the one hand, and ancient or modern thought on the other, can be exactly true. We can only say that, in general, certain lines of thought do particularly characterise one or other of these three periods.

The barbarians who overran the Roman Empire had been, as a rule, strongly individualistic. The Northern tribes were mostly forest-dwellers, who lived mainly by hunting and fishing and rearing cattle, and of whom only the most civilised had reached the stage of settled agriculture. With them, the village was the main political unit; they recognised more vaguely a large agglomeration answering roughly to the modern county; only at times of great crisis was the individual called upon to recognise his duty towards the whole tribe or nation. Again, the Mongol invaders from the East were more individualistic still; certain differences of rank were vaguely recognised; but the Mongol's boast was, "We have no King and we want none; among us every man is King". Still, the invaders had outgrown this extreme individualism to some extent, even before they broke in upon the Empire; indeed, unless they had learned already, by that time, to strike with something of the force of a united nation, and even with the force of different nationalities bound together for the moment by one fixed purpose, they could never have broken the Roman armies. The earliest and most civilised of these invaders, the Goths, recognised very clearly the value of a superior civilisation. They did not aspire to break down the Roman machine, or to replace it by social machinery of their own, but, at first, merely to make for themselves a place in this great civilisation; and, even later, when their military successes had been greatest, they tried to keep as much of the old system as they felt themselves able to work. The highly developed imperial system of taxation and finance was too complicated for them, so that there were no State taxes in the Western Empire for six or seven centuries, until the Crusades again imposed more constructive methods upon the governments; for six or seven centuries rulers had to live and work upon the income of their own royal estates, upon the forced services which they could demand from their subjects in military service, in building of fortifications and of bridges, and upon such booty as they could gain in war. This, as much as anything else, contributed to make war a normal condition of medieval society.

Meanwhile, however, a new civilisation was growing up among the ruins of the old. This was the feudal system—or, as some would cynically call it, want of system. Cynically, I say, for that seems to ignore the essential fact that, however unsystematic feudalism may have been in comparison with the highly developed bureaucracy of the Roman Empire—the too highly developed bureaucracy, most people would say—yet it was systematic as compared with the very primitive way in which the invaders had lived among their native forests and morasses. We may say, roughly, that feudalism was a natural fusion between such new

3

Teutonic elements and such ancient Roman elements as were best suited to coalesce with each other. Already, before the invasions, Roman society had begun in some ways to disintegrate; at the same time, Teutonic society was crystallising into something far more civilised than it had been; this made coalition easier when the time came for a conquering Teutonic population to settle down with a conquered population of Roman traditions.

The bond in feudalism was double, economic and personal. As I have said before, one man was not only owner of another's land, but also master of his person. The tendency in this direction, during the later generations of the Empire, was mainly due to the extent to which the laborious and steady middle classes, the backbone of society, were being exploited. State taxation was elaborate; in some ways it was most ingenious and efficient; but it gradually evolved a great injustice. The great man could often shirk his full burden by bribery or intimidation; the smallest men escaped because it would not have paid to press them; thus the main burden fell upon the peasant-farmers. These men were compelled, in increasing numbers, to shelter themselves under the protection of the nearest great landowner. The great man said, naturally enough: "I can protect my own land, but not other men's. Give me your land and you shall have it back at a small rent". Thus there grew up what the law recognised as *precarial* tenure; tenure under which the tiller of the soil had rights as against other men, but none as against

4

the great man to whom the land had been yielded. We may often see something analogous in modern society. A minister or a philanthropic lay-worker starts a boys' cricket or football club. He goes to the owner of a building-plot that is still vacant, and gets provisional leave for his boys to play there. Those boys and their director have rights as against all other comers, but none whatever as against the owner, who can at any moment withdraw his permission.

Again, Teutonic society had recognised very definitely a personal tie, quite apart from family ties or State ties, between man and man. Young men would attach themselves to some great warrior, to eat at his table and to fight his battles, and this "companionship" as it was called—"vassalage", as we should call it— was recognised as a tie even stronger than that of son to father, or of subject to sovereign. Roman society, also, from very early times, had recognised voluntary ties of this kind, under the title of *patrocinium*, or patronage. If those customs were already vigorous on both sides of the frontier before the invasion, we may easily see how the invasions would have consecrated and developed them. Now, far more than before, the small man needed help, and was willing almost to sell his soul for help, and the great man was able to make a very profitable bargain.

Thus grew up a state of society which lasted for many centuries, and which was at its fullest development about the time of the Norman invasion of England, among those Western Franks, those inhabitants of what we now call France, from whom the Normans had learned most of their own civilisation. It was a great advantage for England that feudalism was thus introduced among us in a more systematic and orderly form than it assumed in some other parts of Europe.

Under the Feudal System, therefore, society was organised very differently from what it had been under the Roman Empire, or from what it is now. Whatever might be the theory, in fact a man's immediate obedience was to his landlord. He might have only one landlord, for the royal estates were considerable, and on those estates the peasant owed homage to the king alone. But, on the other hand, he might have half-a-dozen landlords, in various degrees of proximity. If his immediate landlord was the lord of the manor—the local squire, to put it into modern terms—then that squire might be the direct tenant of the king; but, on the other hand, this squire might hold his lands under some other squire, and he under some other, and he under some count or baron or bishop or abbot, so that there were many steps between the actual tiller of the soil and the central government. But the man's immediate loyalty was due to his immediate landlord; he might have many lords but he had only one *liege* lord, the man from whom he held directly. Thus came about the strange paradox, that the peasant owed closer loyalty to his squire than to his king. Nearly all quarrels were settled in the squire's court, the court of the manor; it is true that if a serf were actually killed or maimed, there was a possible appeal to the king's court; otherwise the man and his master must fight it out for themselves. The Roman Empire had been highly centralised; the Middle Ages were strongly decentralised.

Meanwhile, however, a great central power was growing up. During the decay of the Roman Empire—for decay had definitely set in before that final catastrophe of barbarian invasions—during that decay, then, one thing had been growing stronger, and that was the Christian religion. There may be many different ways of explaining the fact; but it is a fact, as undeniable as any other in history, that this belief in a crucified carpenter and in continued communion with Him through sacraments which He instituted, has taken more men out of themselves, and taken them further out of themselves, than any other event in the world's records, not even excepting Buddhism. The Imperial government had feared and hated this new sect, as a state within the State. But the new religion grew under persecution; and at last Constantine, seeing that he could not stamp it out, chose it for his ally. It became the State Church, while all other creeds were tolerated, if at all, only as superstitions. But presently other creeds were no longer tolerated, and the Church, from being a persecuted sect pleading for mercy, became a powerful organisation, in the face of which others pleaded too often in vain. Before the Empire broke up, this Church had already grown to maturity and vigour. Its organisation, its dress, and even some of its ceremonies were modelled on those of the Empire; it had imitated on a great scale as the Salvation Army has imitated on a smaller scale. It amassed rich endowments, but a very large proportion of these were employed upon charitable or spiritual purposes. Even the barbarians, in their better moments, respected the Church. Therefore, while the civil magistrates were swept away by the invasions, the bishop and the priest remained, as a rule, at their posts. The Church had taken the mould of the Empire, as a hermit-crab takes the mould of its shell; and by about A.D. 700 it may be said that the Roman Church is almost all that remains of the Roman Empire; for, from generation to generation, the Bishop of Rome had gradually obtained a supremacy, more or less definitely recognised, over all other bishops. Thus, in a very real sense, practical form had been given to that theory of the City of God which St Augustine had worked out while the City of Man, the Empire, was visibly going to pieces. That ideal, to which we must come back in a later chapter, dominated nearly all of the thought of the Middle Ages, though not so much of the practice.

The Middle Ages started with certain advantages here, and certain disadvantages. The advantages were mainly two: they started to a great extent with a clean slate; and behind them they had the driving force of the new religion, Christianity. Gibbon would not have counted these as advantages; it is plain that to his mind the coming of Christianity was the first and most fatal of the barbarian victories. He sneers at the boast of the early Christian father Tertullian (*c.* A.D. 220) that a Christian mechanic is ready with answers to questions which had puzzled the wisest heads of antiquity. From one point of view this contempt is justified; but from a wider outlook we must count it a real gain for civilisation that the artisan should seriously concern himself at all with these questions, and that he should find an answer which, on the whole, had a definite ethical value. Society in the Roman Empire had grown more and more lifeless. Originality had decayed in literature and in art. The citizen had surrendered many of his political liberties; he was content to commit the defence of the Empire to hired barbarians; the laborious and thrifty middle classes were being crushed out of existence by a system of taxation which threw the heaviest burden upon the willing horse. In the midst of this indifference or decay one thing grew steadily— the new religion.

It had already lost some of its early characteristics by A.D. 400. Its acceptance as the State religion had brought weakness as well as strength; but it still retained much of that force and originality which had marked Christian society as the one thing which would not fit into conventional Roman civilisation; the one thing which claimed a right of making cleavages everywhere in a society which relied for its stability upon a horizontal structure of caste distinctions; the thing which claimed an even stricter allegiance than State loyalty; the thing, therefore, which was marked for

9

persecution in an otherwise tolerant world. All medieval thought is characterised, nominally at least, by the conviction that each man has a soul to save, and that, therefore, salvation is the main end of every human being, not a distant ideal, but the most practical duty that is set before us all.

This revolutionary seed was sown in a soil fresh ploughed by political and social revolution; or, perhaps, it would be a more exact metaphor to say, in fields swept by a great deluge, and left barren for the moment, but rich in virgin soil. This became, in the long run, the second medieval advantage, lamentable as it was at first. The eastern half of the Roman Empire kept its political and social constitution comparatively intact for centuries, and did scarcely more than mark time all that while. The western half was wrecked, but emerged with a vitality which, when once the Dark Ages were passed, soon carried it ahead, even in those arts in which the Greeks had excelled.

Let us now go back to face the disadvantages. These, again, may be distinguished into two; the moral and the material. The latter needs no special emphasis here; the chaos of the Western world is well known. But morally, while Christianity embodied much of the best of ancient thought, it was also alloyed with a great deal of baser metal.

The main threads, before Christ, may be reckoned as four. These were: first, philosophy, containing a great deal of moral teaching, but mainly academic, and failing to touch the ordinary man; secondly, State religion, which the ordinary man professed as a matter of routine, but which did not even pretend to teach morality, being purely ceremonial; thirdly, the cults, mainly of Eastern origin—those, for example, of Cybele, Isis, Serapis, Mithras—of which the last had little moral content, while the others were, in part at least, frankly immoral; and lastly, Judaism, strong in its monotheism, its abhorrence of idolatry and its social cohesion, but too often narrow and intolerant, conceiving Jehovah as a tribal god friendly to Israel and unfriendly to the Gentile. Those four strands were fused by Christianity.

I have already noted what seems to me one of the most unquestionable of all historical facts: the belief in a crucified Jewish carpenter, however it arose, took more men out of themselves, and further out of themselves, than any similar event of which we have record. Many were wholly possessed with the new ideas, deaf to all dissuasion, and ready for any sacrifice; hence that "inflexible and intolerant zeal" which Gibbon notes as one of the main causes for the spread of Christianity. For one who was thus inspired, hundreds were impressed in varying degrees; and thus the new faith tended to absorb much of what was best in all the earlier strands of thought. But there was more than absorption; there was actual coalescence. This living flame fused the hitherto separate wires into one; and it may be said that, for the Middle Ages, thought ran more definitely along a single line than it had ever run before or since in recorded history. This remains true, even when all the qualifications have been noted to which we shall later come.

But, with the strength of the older ideas, this new creed absorbed some of their weaknesses also. Higher thought was vulgarised, in both senses of the Latin word *vulgaris*. On the one hand, it was spread over the whole mass of the population, the *vulgus*. On the other hand, it must needs stoop to conquer; it compromised to some degree with vulgar prejudices and impulses. From paganism it borrowed the custom of image worship, which to the earliest Fathers was abhorrent: Origen (*c.* A.D. 240) insists that no Christian is so uninstructed as to believe that he can raise his thoughts to God by contemplating an image.[1] From the cults it took an enthusiasm which was not always moral. From Judaism it borrowed a narrow intolerance; God's chosen were a fraction of humanity, the rest, "the nations", "the Gentiles", were outside God's covenant. It was ready to adopt the imperial idea of world domination, by force if necessary; but equally it maintained the great and constructive imperial idea of universality.

Where the barbarian invasions swept away the Roman governors and magistrates, they still left the bishop, as a rule, in his see and the priest at his altar; the episcopal and sacerdotal powers were too tenacious and too spiritual to be destroyed. Latin, which had once been the language common to all cultivated folk in the West, was kept up by the permanence of church service books in Latin, and by that translation of the

---

[1] *Contra Celsum,* bk. VII, c. 44.

Bible which, as revised by St Jerome, became the Vulgate, the universally recognised version which practically superseded the original. A few scores of volumes, or, in fortunate instances, even hundreds, remained safe enough in monasteries or in the sacristies of great churches to survive all but the worst inroads of the pirates.

Thus again, Christianity worked for the vulgarisation of knowledge in both senses of the word. On the one hand, it cast overboard, as useless or even noxious, a great deal of what was noblest in ancient thought. The early Fathers were naturally tempted to puritanism here: Tertullian complains that the ancient philosophers are the patriarchs of heresy; St Gregory the Great is scandalised to hear that a bishop is teaching "grammar", that is, the classics, in which the pupil was normally introduced at an early age to Vergil, with his praise of Jove as All-Ruler, and his emphasis on earthly love.[1] Therefore the classical volumes preserved were comparatively few in number and narrow in their range; Cardinal Newman's vision of the medieval monk as a classical scholar is largely imaginary. But, on the other hand, below such exaggerations the fact remains that "narrow as may have been the Churchman's educational ideal, it was only among Churchmen that an educational ideal maintained itself at all. . . . The grossest ignorance of the Dark Ages was not due to the strength of the ecclesiastical system, but to its

[1] *Ep.* IX, 54; cf. R. L. Poole, *Medieval Thought and Learning*, 2nd ed., p. 7.

13

weakness".[1] The little that survived of ancient learning was spread among people far less cultivated than the society they had displaced, yet more energetic and with a fresher outlook.

Just as the Christian religion is (as Dr Warde Fowler has put it) "a plant which, though grown in a soil which has borne other crops, is wholly new in structure and vital principle", so is it with medieval thought. This may be clearly differentiated from either classical thought on the one hand or modern thought on the other. It was, at first, triumphantly conscious of its novelty; in its attitude towards Greece and Rome it was inspired by Tertullian's boast: "We are men of yesterday, yet we have filled your world"—*hesterni sumus, et vestra omnia implevimus*. It was inspired also by the appeal to the individual conscience; "a fugitive glance at medieval doctrine suffices to perceive how throughout it all, in sharp contrast to the theories of antiquity, runs the thought of the absolute and imperishable value of the Individual: a thought revealed by Christianity and grasped in all its profundity by the Germanic spirit".[2] The Middle Ages never altogether lost that tone of the Apocalypse: "Babylon the great is fallen, is fallen.... Come out of her, my people, that ye be not partakers of her sins.... And the Spirit and the bride say, Come.... And let him that is athirst come.... He which testifieth these things saith, Surely I come quickly. Amen. Even so, come, Lord Jesus".

[1] H. Rashdall, *Universities of Europe*, I, 26.
[2] Gierke-Maitland, *Political Theories of the Middle Age*, p. 81.

Though the expectation of the Second Advent receded as time went on, yet it never seemed far beyond the immediate horizon. Treatises on Antichrist abound. Even Roger Bacon, writing in 1271, speaks of the common belief among "wise men" that this last stage of the world is imminent. Dante leaves very few seats to be filled in his Paradise; and, if he could be recalled to earth, he would probably be less surprised at any modern invention, than that the world had lasted 600 years after his death. The same belief meets us again in almost every generation; Sir Thomas More himself was inclined to it. Therefore, while the best medieval thought was deeply serious, and penetrated with the sense of personal responsibility, yet it sometimes suffered from an impatience which was the defect of these qualities; the world-fabric might crash at any moment; what was the use of painfully beginning a long and continuous chain of facts and inferences which involved the labour of whole generations or centuries, when a few years or even weeks might bring the consummation of all things? It is not only the difficulty of writing records and preserving the documents once written, and comparing them by free and constant interchange among students, that explains the painful lack of historical sense, and of scientific observation or experiment in physics and natural history, during this long period. Much was due also to this predominantly other-worldly attitude of mind among many of the greatest thinkers. So far as this world is concerned, "laissez le long espoir et les vastes pensées";

man's first and second and last task is to prepare himself for eternity.

And for what sort of eternity? There again, we cannot even remotely appreciate medieval thought without reminding ourselves of the assumptions from which it started. The contrast frequently drawn by modern writers between medieval and post-Reformation conceptions of biblical infallibility are too often either altogether false or greatly exaggerated. As to the *interpretation* of Bible texts, there is indeed a gulf between the Roman Catholic and the Protestant theory; the former reserves all final judgment to the official Church, while the latter claims each man's right to interpret the text according to his own reason and his own conscience. But, with regard to the *inerrancy* of the written word, it is difficult to find any real distinction. St Thomas Aquinas, following mainly St Augustine, teaches that the author of Holy Writ is God, in Whose power it is to signify His meaning, not by words only (as man also can do), but also by things themselves. It follows, as the first consequence of this authorship, that the Holy Scriptures can never contain an untruth in their literal sense; rather, we must believe all that stands in the Bible as God's Word. For not only all that relates to matters of faith and morals, but its historical contents also are truths sponsored by God. Therefore, if (for instance) anyone said that Samuel was not the son of Elkanah, it would follow that the Divine Scriptures would be false, which would be to contradict the Faith, however indirectly, and therefore

16

to fall into heresy. He is no less explicit on other similar points. We may, indeed, allegorise the Tree of Life as described in Genesis; we may quote from Proverbs iii, 18, to show that it signifies "wisdom"; but this must not in any way prejudice our acceptance of the description in its most literal sense. "We must take for our foundation the truth of the story, and on that foundation we must build our spiritual expositions." Therefore we may not deny the botanical fact of such a tree, or the geographical fact that it stood in the earthly Paradise.[1] Indeed, there are only three heads under which any exception can be made to the full acceptance of all biblical statements in their literal sense: (1) We must make allowance for the weakness of human language and its consequent inability to express the highest thoughts. (2) We must allow also for weakness of understanding on the part of the hearers; thus Moses was obliged to condescend to the Israelites, expressing himself in simple, and therefore not always strictly accurate, terms. (3) The passage, again, may be purely allegorical. But we see from the two instances he himself has given, and from the general practice of the medieval and later Roman Church, how little the tendency to allegorise affected men's insistence upon the literal sense also. Innocent III, writing to demand obedience from the Greek Church, based his claim (*inter alia*) upon two wildly allegorical interpretations. When St Peter leapt into the sea in order to join the risen Lord without delay, and when on a

[1] *Sum. Theol.*, pars 1. quaestt. XXXII and CII.

previous occasion he walked for a moment with Christ on the water, he thereby betokened his right of domination over all mankind, since the ancient gloss on the Psalms interprets "many waters" in the sense of "the whole world".[1] But Innocent, while thus allegorising, would not have suffered the least doubt as to the literal description of Peter's action in either case; and many centuries later, when Galileo was condemned, one of the counts against him was that his theory contradicted that plain statement in the Psalms "He hath established the world, which shall not be moved" —*firmavit orbem terrae, qui non commovebitur* (Ps. xcii, 1, Vulg.; A.V. Ps. xciii, 1).

Thus the medieval Church felt absolutely bound to accept in their strictest sense all Bible texts about heaven and hell; and many circumstances contributed, in those troubled times, to darken that already gloomy picture. St Thomas is at great pains to show that we may not doubt the physical reality of hell-fire; and indeed he expatiates at greater length upon the torments, and with more emphasis, than Calvin, who is sometimes ignorantly credited with a severity which belongs more truly to his medieval predecessors. The fact is that, partly by exaggeration of certain gospel sentences and of traditions inherited from Judaism or borrowed from other religions, partly again under stress of persecution and natural bitterness of mind, Christianity had early developed a very lurid escha-

[1] I give full quotations in the fourteenth of my *Medieval Studies* (3rd ed., p. 9).

tology. Tertullian's fierce anticipations of hell for unbelievers and persecutors have often been quoted; Dante's *Inferno*, again, is familiar to many readers; but Dante is less crude in his expression of the contrasts between heaven and hell than the ordinary preacher of his own or of later time. St Francis of Assisi preached hell as definitely as General Booth. The Franciscan Berthold of Regensburg, whom Roger Bacon extols as the greatest mission-preacher of that day, recurs constantly to this subject. Here is a brief summary with references to volume and page of Pfeiffer's standard edition.

The sinner suffers as many deaths as the motes that dance in the sun (II, 2). If thy whole body were of red-hot iron, and the whole world, from earth to heaven, one vast fire, and thou in the midst, that is how a man is in hell, except that he is an hundredfold worse (I, 127). And when, at the Last Day, soul and body are united again, and the two together must go back to hell, then will the damned feel it as much worse as the plunge from cool dew into a mountain of fire (II, 40). The tortures will endure as many thousand years as there are drops in the sea, or as the number of all the hairs that have grown on man and beast since God first made Adam; and then, after all those years, the pains will only be at their beginning (I, 72).

To this hell the majority of the human race went. That was taken for granted; it is accepted even by St Thomas Aquinas, who among all medieval philosophers is specially remarkable for his balance of judgment; other writers often reckon the saved as only one in a thousand, or in ten thousand, or in more. Unbaptised children, and pagans, however virtuous, must go to hell; Dante's two exceptions prove the rule; as for the rest (although he forsakes Augustine and follows Aquinas in rejecting the idea of bodily torture) the air is thick with their sighs and groans. All orthodox medieval thought rested upon the assumption that the last moment of life marked the man for an eternity of unspeakable bliss or of torment beyond all conception. And, as this was decided by the dying man's state at that last moment, so the decisive factor in this state was his theological belief. The enormous significance of these fundamental assumptions will become more apparent later on.

Again, in the Dark Ages, we must not neglect the influence of that paganism—Teutonic, Celtic, Slavonic—which the Church did indeed conquer, but partly by compromise. She found infanticide in a certain sense legalised among the Frisians of the eighth century and the Icelanders of the eleventh; in this latter case, she even compounded for a while. She taught the worship of St Vitus to the pagans of the Isle of Rügen; and a few generations later, in the mid-twelfth century, the saint's statue had become an idol which the natives called Suantovit, and to which they occasionally offered human sacrifices, "but only of Christian folk". Gregory the Great, in his advice to the missionaries whom he had sent to convert the English heathen, emphasised the necessity of compromise on inessential points; let the old temples be baptised to the new Church uses, let heathen festivals be retained, but let them be diverted from the worship of devils to that of the true God. Such compromises were doubtless wise and necessary, yet they bore their inevitable fruit; and, together with pagan customs, many pagan ideas sheltered themselves under the wing of the medieval Church.

CHAPTER II

The Medieval Village

THROUGHOUT this little book, the examples will be most often drawn from English social history; but, in default of notice to the contrary, the reader may take them as typical of European society in general.

The Teutons, like the Mongols, had been in many ways strongly democratic. In the village meeting there were certain precedences of honour, but in the strictest theory all grown-up warriors were considered as essentially equal. Probably a great many talked at once; certainly approval or disapproval were shown loudly, and in great part by the clashing of swords and spears and shields. Therefore the side which felt itself weaker gradually gave way, and the theory of Teutonic law was that the decision had been unanimous. This theory still survives in our jury system. And what I have said of the village meeting may be said also of those meetings, naturally more important and rarer, which were attended by a whole county (as we should now call it) or a whole tribe.

This theoretical equality of all freemen naturally involved something like an equal partition of the village lands; and indeed, in most cases, a redistribution from year to year. This was easy enough before the tribes had arrived at a settled agricultural civilisation, and it remained possible even after that stage. The Norman Conquest, therefore, found England not yet entirely emerged from this stage; there were definite survivals of the primitive equal distribution of land. The normal peasant holding was a *virgate* or yard-land; as much as a man and his family could till properly with two oxen; this naturally varied with the nature of the soil. The average was about thirty acres, but we sometimes find a good deal more or less. We learn a great deal about the peasant from Domesday Book, a business record drawn up for purposes of taxation by orders of William the Conqueror, which still survives as the most valuable record of its kind and of its age in the whole world. This record shows us how large a proportion of the population were actual slaves, and how numerous, again, was the semi-slave class, the serfs. This intermediate class increased, in proportion as the extreme classes of slaves at one end, and freemen at the other, diminished. The slaves, we are glad to think, diminished most in the long run; slavery was not only unphilanthropical but uneconomical, as a general rule. Domesday shows us, on one manor, a drop from eighty-two slaves to twenty-five in the preceding twenty years. In England slavery proper was dead before the thirteenth century. In Spain, Southern France, and Italy it flourished all through the Middle Ages; and in the Papal States it was rather increasing than dying when our period ends. More than one Pope, in the later Middle Ages, decreed slavery as a punishment for his political enemies; and the negro slave-trade had its legal origin in two Papal bulls.[1] But in England, at any rate, the slave's gain proved to some extent the freeman's loss. Lords wanted cheap labour, and they too often took advantage of their position to obtain it by force or by sharp practice. Mr William Hudson, who has done most valuable and disinterested antiquarian work, has worked out with marvellous patience a precious series of details from the records of a Norfolk manor, Martham in the Norfolk Broads. There, as in all districts much affected by the Danish invasions, the proportion of freemen in Domesday is large; the peasants were descendants of the conquering Danes. There were seventy-eight freemen to only seven serfs. But the Norman bishops of Norwich, to whom the manor went, reduced sixty-five out of the seventy-eight freemen to servile status. In the county of Cambridge, again, there were 900 freemen at the Conquest and, twenty years later, only 213.

This dispossession of freemen went on during the first part of our period far more rapidly than the extinction of slavery proper. By the middle of our period—in Chaucer's day, for instance—less than half the population of these islands were freemen.

The village was the political and ecclesiastical unit; the agricultural unit was the manor. Often village and manor were co-extensive; but often there were two or more manors in one village. Look up your own village in the County History, or ask some local antiquarian, and you will probably learn the names of

[1] See my *Medieval Village*. pp. 171, 495 ff.

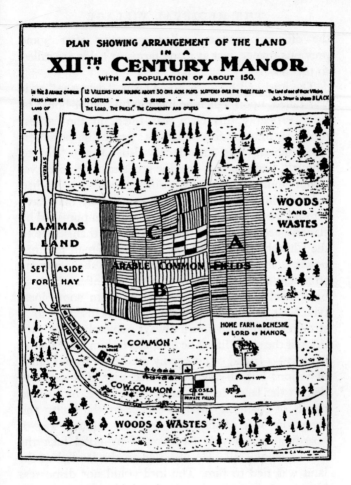

PLAN SHOWING ARRANGEMENT OF THE LAND
IN A
XIITH CENTURY MANOR
WITH A POPULATION OF ABOUT 150.

IN THE 8 ARABLE COMMON | 12 VILLEINS. EACH HOLDING ABOUT 30 ONE ACRE PLOTS SCATTERED OVER THE THREE FIELDS. | The Land of one of these Villeins
FIELDS MIGHT BE | 10 COTTERS " " 3 OR MORE " " SIMILARLY SCATTERED & | Jack Straw is shewn BLACK
LAND OF | THE LORD, THE PRIEST, THE COMMUNITY and OTHERS " " |

WOODS
AND
WASTES

LAMMAS
LAND

SET ASIDE
FOR HAY

C

A

ARABLE COMMON FIELDS

B

HOME FARM or DEMESNE
of LORD of MANOR

COMMON

JACK STRAW'S HOUSE

COW COMMON

CLOSES
or PRIVATE FIELDS

WOODS & WASTES

25

the different manors, called generally after some previous owner, just as many farms or fields are called to this day.

The lord had his own home farm, "demesne" as it was called, upon which he lived in his manor-house or hall. Probably this farm was tilled, in the earliest times, entirely by forced labour; gradually, however, hired labour was introduced also. I say "forced labour", because that was the serf's rent. A medieval writer enumerates for us the different causes which had led men into bondage; first, he says, they may have refused when called out for war, and been punished by slavery; secondly, they may have given themselves to the Church; thirdly, by sale, as when a man fell into poverty, and said unto some lord: "Ye shall give me so much, and I shall become your man of my body"; or fourthly, to defend themselves from some local tyrant or enemy they had given themselves to a stronger man. We must always remember the two sides of the serf's life. The lord was to him what nature is to us—a friend or an enemy according to our angle of vision; but, in any case, a necessity. The serf was tied to the land; in England, at any rate, he had no means of changing masters except by the guilty and dangerous way of flight, or the very difficult way of hoarding and buying freedom, if by good luck the master would sell. He was tied to the land; but the land was tied to him. The lord could not dispossess him except for refusal to render the legal dues, or for some other equally good reason.

These legal dues were originally quite simple; the peasant held his land on condition of working three days of the week for his master and three for himself. Sunday work was strictly forbidden; the Church, in theory, was as Sabbatarian as many of those later people whom we call Puritans with regard to labour, and sometimes even with regard to amusements. There are instances on both sides. (i) The Franciscan Archbishop Odo Rigaldi of Rouen notes in his diary for 1260 how he found ploughs at work on St Matthew's Day, and impounded the horses until the owners should pay whatever fine he imposed; four years later, on a Sunday, he found a carter at work, and fined him ten *sols*, or about three weeks' wages.[1] (ii) Medieval moralists frequently quote a sentence from St Augustine which they interpret in the sense that even to work on a Sunday or holy-day is one degree less sinful than to dance. Again, pious priests not only discouraged this amusement, but often actually forbade it; we may find preachers condemning it as a mortal sin.[2] Here, however, as elsewhere in the Middle Ages, there was a great gulf between theory and practice; we have strong evidence that the peasants very frequently broke the rule of *sabbatizare* (as the theological phrase went) in both directions. Moralists complain abundantly of the amount of work that was often done, and the busy markets that went on, in spite of Sunday or holy-day; and superabundantly they tell us of the direct ratio

[1] *Medieval Village*, p. 256; cf. pp. 530 ff.
[2] *Ibid.* pp. 559 ff.

between holy-days and all kinds of amusements, both legal and illegal. When Henry VIII's government of 1536 proposed the suppression of superfluous holy-days, this was only a tardy recognition of what had long since been insisted upon by the theologians, that more laws were broken on Sundays and Saints' days than in the rest of the week.

Certain other dues, originally voluntary to please the lord, became so customary that they finally became binding in law, just as our hotel tips have now become a statutory 10 per cent. Gradually, however, it became evident to both lord and serf that a money payment was generally the best bargain for both parties. But in Chaucer's day serfdom was the commonest status: the lord's demesne was cultivated partly by forced labour and partly by hired labour, paid for by the money which some serfs rendered for their commutations. And the whole agriculture, whether on the demesne or on the rest of the manor, was carried on sometimes by the two-field system, far more frequently by the three-field. The whole arable land was divided into two, or into three, fields. By the former system the only rotation of crops was the simple change from corn to fallow in alternate years. By the latter there were three variations: in the first year wheat was sown; next year, barley; and the third year the field lay fallow and rested.

Medieval agriculture was necessarily to some extent communal; as to the exact extent, men are still disputing. Holdings had, no doubt, been compact at

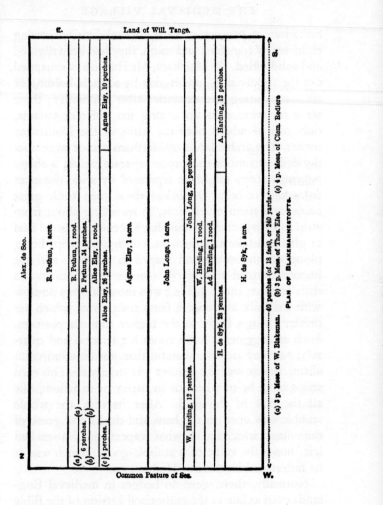

PLAN OF BLAKEMANNESTOFTE.

(a) 3 p. Mess. of Will. Blakeman.   (b) 3 p. Mess. of Thos. Else.   (c) 4 p. Mess. of Clem. Redlers

first; but in process of time, by subdivision among children, by transfers, and so on, they had been divided and subdivided. At Martham, Mr Hudson has mapped out the subdivisions undergone by a single holding of six acres during two centuries after Domesday; these six acres were split up among ten different tenants, only one of whom bore the name of the Domesday owner. The arable lands of Martham manor were now divided into more than 2000 separate strips; a single peasant's strips might be separated by wide distances from each other. Doubtless these men took great pains, and spent much time, in travelling about from strip to strip; yet there must have been also a good deal of give-and-take arrangement, contiguous strips being ploughed and sown and reaped in a block, and the harvest divided among the owners in proportion to their acreage; much as the Swiss mountaineers do now with the milk and cheese from their cows, which are driven up in a body to the higher summer pastures. Such arrangements leave room for friction and quarrels; yet they are less wasteful than absolute individualism. In one way the peasant was strictly tied; his own strips must be in wheat or in barley or in fallow, like all the rest of the field. After harvest, the whole stubble was open to the hens and ducks and geese of the village, which fed on what reapers and gleaners had left; hence the value of a stubble-goose, which was at its fattest and best about Michaelmas.

Normally, there were no hedges in medieval England; even as late as the authorised version of the Bible this comes out; Isaac goes out at evening not into the *fields* (plural), but into the *field* (singular). Each cottage had normally its little fenced toft and garden; again, the best meadow-land was fenced, that it might be kept for hay: but in the great stretch of arable land the strips were divided from each other only by balks, or narrow lines of turf. This great-field system survives here and there in England to the present day; but, as a rule, to see what the medieval landscape looked like, we must go abroad; let us say, to the Norman valleys round Dieppe, which in natural conformation resemble Kent and Sussex, yet are in many ways so different.

Besides the arable, and besides the fenced hay-meadows, there was always a good deal of rough pasture, common-land on which the peasants had grazing rights; also a certain amount of wood, in which the village had certain rights for fuel or fencing-sticks or sometimes for building-timber, but no sporting rights; game-preserving was even stricter in Chaucer's England than in Fielding's.

The three main manorial officials were agricultural. The lord's right-hand-man was his steward or bailiff, who presided in the manor court. Equally necessary was the *praepositus*, or reeve, elected yearly, and nominally a representative of the tenants, but in fact tempted to maintain the lord's interests almost as definitely as the bailiff. Thirdly, there was the hayward, who did in fact guard the hay, though that syllable is only a corruption of his original name, *Heggeward*. It was his duty to see that no beast broke through hedges

into hayfield or corn or some other man's toft; any
stray cattle that he found were clapped into the village
pound, which sometimes still exists. Even in a borough
like King's Lynn, the pound was still in existence fifty
years ago. A fourth officer, less formal than those
other three, was needed at harvest-time; this was the
superior peasant who, as one condition of his tenure,

The Overseer's Rod
(from Queen Mary's Psalter)

had to "hold his rod over the reapers", for the serf
might be beaten by the lord or the lord's officers, so
long as the chastisement stopped short of grievous
bodily harm. The village must have its smith also, if
not voluntarily, then by compulsion; for he was
absolutely necessary to the community, and the carpenter almost as necessary. The tailor was far less
common; the village shopkeeper was absolutely non-
existent. What men ate and drank and wore was

home-grown, and often home-made, down to the last crumb or drop or stitch. What could not be made in the village was obtained in the market or fair of the nearest town; Chaucer's peasant might be described exactly as Virgil describes his own Italian peasant, taking his produce down into the town and coming back with a

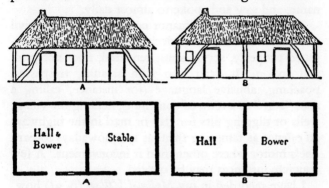

A Cottage of about 1300
(from a contemporary specification, which answers
either to (A) or to (B))

grindstone or a stock of pitch: "Often doth the driver of the slow-moving ass load his back with oil-jars or with cheap apples, and, returning from the town, bring back a grindstone or a mass of swarthy pitch" (*Georgics* I, 273).

Indeed, we need an effort of imagination to grasp how self-sufficing, and therefore how isolated, the medieval countryside was. The average village contained only about 400 souls; let us say, 250 adults at most, probably less, and 150 children. All these people, normally, lived their whole lives in the village and saw very few folk from outside. Therefore, apart from stray and momentary passers by, these men and women went from the cradle to the grave in company with about as many adults as could be carried in four London omnibuses, every one of whom they knew by name, and saw and spoke to almost daily.

The business of the medieval manor court was double—civil and criminal. The court decided all questions of disputed property, services not rendered, fines not paid, and so on. It dealt also with assaults, trespasses, poaching, abusive language (for instance, calling a man "serf" as a term of contempt), defiling the village wells or digging pits for clay or marl in the highway; an offence as tempting then, as it is nowadays to park one's motor where others find it inconvenient. A few concrete instances may be quoted.

I have recorded in my *Medieval Village* (p. 91) how as early as 1364 we find the injunction "upon all the tenants of East Raynton and West Raynton that none of them shall call any man of either manor 'a serf of the lord prior', under pain of 20*s*. upon the offender". In 1365, at Newton Beaulieu, a fine of 6*s*. 8*d*. is decreed against anyone who calls another *rusticum*; at the same court, John of Bamborough was in fact presented for calling Adam of Marton "false, perjured and *rustic*, to the damage of the said Adam". But the fine actually adjudged was only 3*s*. 4*d*.; and, finally, "of mercy", only a single shilling was taken from John. In 1378, again, the tenants of Wolveston were threatened with a fine of 20*s*. for any man who "should call any serf of my lord prior *rusticum*". *Rusticus* was often used as a synonym of *servus* or *villanus*.

On the next page (92) I have given references for presentments as to pits on the highway; but the most interesting of all is quoted by Mrs J. R. Green in her *Town Life in the Fifteenth Century*, II, 31:

In 1499 a glover from Leighton Buzzard travelled with his wares to Aylesbury for the market before Christmas Day. It happened that an Aylesbury miller, Richard Boose, finding that his mill needed repairs, sent a couple of servants to dig clay "called Ramming clay" for him on the highway, and was in no way dismayed because the digging of this clay made a great pit in the middle of the road ten feet wide, eight feet broad and eight feet deep, which was quickly filled with water by the winter rains. But the unhappy glover, making his way from the town in the dusk, with his horse laden with paniers full of gloves, straightway fell into the pit and the man and horse were drowned. The miller was charged with his death, but was acquitted by the court on the ground that he had had no malicious intent, and had only dug the pit to repair his mill, and because he really did not know of any other place to get the kind of clay he wanted save the highroad.

As to the quarrels which occupied so much of the business in these village courts, they arose sometimes from drink or from inter-village football, played with medieval vigour and freedom from discipline; sometimes, again, from old family feuds, but most frequently, to all appearance, from the women's tongues. At Billingham, in Northumberland or Durham, the court "ordains by common consent that all the women of the township control their tongues, without any sort of defamation". At Hazeldean, again, in 1375 "it was enjoined upon all the women in the township that they should restrain their tongues and not scold nor curse any man".[1]

Manor court procedure retained many traces of primitive democracy. The judgment was given, in form at least, by the tenants themselves, who, on oath, decided according to the customs of the manor. Different manors had their different customs; scarcely any two manor customals will be found exactly identical; the differences of detail are often important and yet all bear a strong family likeness, the stamp of a society which differed widely from our own. And, in spite of the democratic forms, all chances weighed heavily in the lord's favour, even when the reeve was not as definitely his man as the bailiff was. It was a primitive, patriarchal society compared with our own, but that meant that things depended enormously upon the patriarch; upon the squire, or, in many cases, upon his officers. For a distinguished ecclesiastic of Chaucer's day, the Dominican Bromyard, tells us that the petty tyrant of the fields was often the bailiff, who might get everything into his own hands under a good-natured easy-going lord, and who might thus fleece the villagers in order to please his master with an increase of income.

[1] These and other similar details may be found on pp. 92 ff. of my *Medieval Village*.

CHAPTER III

The Church and the Village

WE may characterise medieval village government not unfairly as squirearchy, though often a benevolent squirearchy enough, just as the squirearchy of the eighteenth century was often benevolent also. On the lay side, medieval village government was decidedly paternal; and it was still more paternal on the side of the Church, which was then of enormous importance.

Such civilisation as these people possessed came, to a very large extent, through the clergy. The Roman Church was in some real sense the legitimate heir of the Roman Empire. For many centuries churchmen were almost the only persons who wrote or read books. In all countries north of the Alps they had the legal monopoly of all teaching, from the University down to the elementary school. There was not, in fact, any regular educational system in the Middle Ages, though this is sometimes wrongly asserted nowadays. In theory there was what we should call a theological college in every cathedral city; and this was generally fulfilled in practice also, though the students were seldom numerous. Again, we very occasionally find bishops or church councils, once even a Pope, prescribing that each priest should teach gratuitously in his own parish; but there is abundant evidence that this remained a pious aspiration. In the later Middle Ages we often find the parish clerk teaching a few children for small fees; later still, a good many chantry priests, whose only duty at first had been to sing one Mass every morning, were compelled to keep school also; so that the country undoubtedly suffered for a time, at the Reformation, by the suppression of those small schools. Twice, in fifteenth-century London, attempts were made to increase the school accommodation, but with small success owing to the clerical monopolists. The assertion that the monks were educators of the general population is now abandoned by the best scholars of all creeds; they very seldom taught outside boys except under missionary conditions. Nuns, however, did sometimes teach a very few of the richer girls in order to eke out their poor endowments; but this was often discouraged, and sometimes even forbidden, by their ecclesiastical superiors.[1] It is improbable that even one-tenth of the medieval population had had any schooling whatever.

Religious teaching, naturally enough, was monopolised by the Church; yet even here the monopolists were far less active than they are generally represented. Exceptionally pious priests unquestionably evangelised their parishioners, not only in word but by their

[1] I deal fully with this subject in the tenth of my Medieval Studies, *Monastic Schools in the Middle Ages.*

example; witness Chaucer's immortal Poor Parson. But there is no trace of anything even remotely resembling the Sunday school. At the end of the thirteenth century, in consequence of a great religious revival, it was proclaimed by the Archbishop of Canterbury that every parish priest must preach at least four times a year, and must, in those four sermons, expound the Creed, the Ten Commandments, the Sermon on the Mount, the Seven Deadly Sins, the Seven Main Virtues, the Seven Works of Mercy and the Seven Sacraments. Yet not only was this an innovation, but the ecclesiastical records show how little the proclamation was obeyed; and here readers must beware of the too frequent assertion that the deficiencies which I have indicated were fully supplied by church pictures and carvings. The church walls were the poor man's Bible: that is true up to a certain point. But the best churchmen themselves, in the Middle Ages, confess how little a picture can make up for the lack of serious teaching; and, in fact, we have only to look for ourselves at the fragments which remain in our churches, in order to realise how small a proportion of these pictures were Biblical at all.

I have twice used the word *monopoly* as expressing one necessary side of the truth, though far from the whole truth. That was the seamy side, if you choose, of the medieval Church's *universality*. Every child was baptised into that Church; or, if baptism were wilfully omitted, there was presumption of heresy against the parents. All nonconformity was heresy, and all pertinacious nonconformity was punishable with the stake.[1] The cleric's power extended far beyond what we should call purely spiritual, or even intellectual, matters. Beyond his monopoly of religious and non-religious teaching, and the immense social and political power which he derived from the confessional, he had the right of judging and punishing in all important moral questions—usury, witchcraft and everything connected with the marriage laws. If a parishioner had not already made his will in writing—which not one in a hundred did—then he must make it orally to the priest on his deathbed; this was included by implication among those last ceremonies of the Church which, if neglected, deprived the corpse of any right to the consecrated graveyard and to the Church's prayers. The cleric's person was sacred; no ordinary confessor might absolve the man who had wilfully assaulted even the parish clerk, let alone the priest. His goods and chattels shared to a considerable extent in the sacredness which attached to his person. Every church was a sanctuary in which the felon might take refuge from justice, for forty days at least. Finally, Church dues, to which we must return later, formed a very conspicuous feature in every man's life.

There is general agreement now among historians as to the origin of the parish, in its main outlines. The parochial system was not created from above, by the Pope or the hierarchy; rather, it grew up from below,

[1] See the nineteenth of my Medieval Studies, *The Death Penalty for Heresy*, and my volume in Benn's Sixpenny Series on *The Inquisition*.

by natural evolution from pre-Christian conditions. In pagan times the lord had the right of building a temple, exacting religious dues, and appointing the priest. The system worked, and it was naturally carried on into Christian times. The lords had not always dealt honestly with the money thus raised; a good deal of it had sometimes stuck to their fingers. But William the Conqueror earned special praise from Pope Gregory VII for his zeal in defending Church rights here; and, in England, the tithes seem to have gone almost entirely, if not to the priest, at least to the Church. I say "if not to the priest" because, when we study any particular parish church, especially towards the end of our period, we shall find, almost as likely as not, that the priest was losing a great proportion of his tithes. This brings me to the distinction, so often puzzling to modern enquirers, between rectories and vicarages. Why, for instance, is the parish priest of Great Shelford in Cambridgeshire only a vicar, while the priest of Little Shelford is a rector and has a larger income for 500 people than his neighbour has for 1500? The answer is, briefly, because Great Shelford has been robbed of what are called the Great Tithes (mainly tithes of corn and similar crops) while Little Shelford has not.

The fact is that, as village prosperity and general civilisation improved, the tithes and other Church dues, in a large number of parishes, amounted to a good deal more than the mere bachelor priest needed for a living wage, even if we use that phrase in its most generous sense. That was one thing which tempted the lords to embezzle a share of the tithes. Where the Church was strong (as it was in Norman England, partly through the merits of the churchmen themselves, and partly through William's protection), there it was possible to put an end to laymen's robberies; but that which was disgorged did not go back to the parish; on the contrary, that and a great deal more went to monasteries or cathedrals or other great religious corporations. Just then was about the most efficient period of monastic life; the monks, on the whole, were the pick of the ecclesiastical population, and deservedly the most popular. Therefore some lords during their own lifetime, and far more by their deathbed dispositions, gave up to monasteries those churches which they possessed because their ancestors had founded them. At first, this gift was not so very advantageous from the pecuniary stand-point; it only meant that the priest was now appointed, not by the original lord but by the monastery, and that the monks, by bargaining with him, might get pickings from the revenues. But, about the time our period begins, popes and bishops had begun to allow the monks, in specially privileged cases, to take the church *in proprios usus*—to "appropriate" it, as the term soon ran. In such cases the legal position was this: the monastery was rector—that is, ruler—of the parish, with right to all the tithes and other dues. But monks seldom did priestly duties in the parishes; in fact, papal decisions formally forbade this during most of our period.

Therefore the monks put in a curate to do the actual parish duty. For such a curate (as for all substitutes in any walk of life) the natural Latin name was *Vicarius*. Gradually these "appropriations" multiplied; we can trace in the documents by what means, and to what extent, monasteries were willing to pay heavily for the favour of an appropriation both to their diocesan bishop and to the Pope. Before the Reformation, about one-third of the livings in England had thus become vicarages; the incumbent, in those cases, was just a perpetual curate, with such shares of the income as he could manage to get. By that time popes and bishops had interfered in the interests of the vicars, and had insisted upon, at least, a bare living wage for them. The regular proportion was for the appropriator to take two-thirds of the income, leaving the remaining third to the man who did the work. But Pope Innocent III refers to cases in which the vicar received only one-sixteenth of the whole parish income. In these circumstances it was the poor who suffered most. By Church theory, one-quarter of the parish income was earmarked for the poor; and attempts were sometimes made to remind appropriators of this rule. But there was no machinery whatever for enforcing it upon the parish clergy; and, though Parliament did intervene and struggle to enforce it to some extent upon the appropriators, yet Bromyard, that Dominican friar who was Chaucer's contemporary, tells us that it was very generally neglected.

However, at the very worst, the Church was the

main centre of village life. By this time it was a definite clause of the orthodox creed that the unworthiness of a minister does not affect the efficiency of the Sacraments which he administers; to assert that it does had been condemned as definitely heretical. The fabric of the village church, its ornaments and all the things that it stood for were hallowed by long and noble associations. The clergy, even at their least efficient stage, were as a body better educated and more personally respectable than the average of their parishioners. The spiritual protection which they offered, though it might be quite as far from perfection as was the squire's material protection, was yet real. Apart from the more important Church services and the Sacraments, there were exorcisms at every turn against evil spirits and sorcery. The church bells were tolled against the approaching storms, which had been

Witches brewing a Hailstorm

conjured by some witch; and the priest would sometimes formally curse, with sprinklings of holy water, a plague of caterpillars or locusts. Villagers felt at home within the four walls of the church, and the difficulty was rather to prevent too great familiarity. Church councils had to forbid theatrical performances and dances and semi-religious beer-drinkings within the church or its precincts, and to prohibit markets in the churchyard. Here, moreover, the clergy themselves sometimes set an example of freedom, stacking corn or even brewing beer in the nave of their church. Here, for instance, is the report on St Marychurch, near Torquay, by the official deputed to visit the Dean and Chapter livings in 1301.

The parishioners report that the Vicar puts his beasts of all kinds in the churchyard, whereby it is evilly trodden and foully defiled. *Item*, the said Vicar takes to himself, and uses for his own buildings, the trees that fall down in the churchyard. *Item*, the said Vicar has his malt made [*or*, *possibly*, his beer brewed] in the church, and stores his corn and other things therein; whereby his servants, in their going and coming, open the door; and in time of storm the wind comes in and is wont to uncover the church [*i.e.* to blow the tiles or the thatch about].[1]

Yet, with all that, the church and its graveyard were certainly the most decorous corners of the parish; they afforded guidance to the living and comfort to the dying. In so far as society had struggled out of its earlier barbarism, and had regained something of classical civilisation; in so far as it had gone farther and had reached in some directions a higher level than the Greeks and Romans, this was mainly due to the Church. But her undeniable spiritual services must not be emphasised without the corresponding and

[1] *Bp Stapeldon's Register*, ed. Hingeston-Randolph, p. 337.

equally undeniable fact that her jealous exclusiveness suffered no rival spiritual services; you must accept the clergy, such as they were, or quit this world altogether. Therefore the clergy, such as they were, would have been decidedly better if they had had less of a monopoly. Dante was not the only medieval thinker who felt that the Church would have been truly stronger if Constantine had given her less of worldly power.

She was ubiquitous in the mere number of her officers. Below the clergy in "major orders" or "holy orders"—that is, sub-deacons, deacons, and priests, with the higher prelates above them, all of whom were legally unable to marry—below these, there was a whole multitude of "clerks in minor orders", who were not forbidden to marry, and who lived by small jobs such as singing the minor services, acting as parish clerks, or keeping business accounts. It is among these minor clerics that we must seek the majority of the men who wrote the manor rolls for which Thorold Rogers gives credit to the manorial bailiffs. Many of these men earned money by trading, in spite of frequent ecclesiastical prohibitions; some sold drink; some actually throve upon usury, which was mortal sin even for a layman. I do not think we can reckon the clergy, of all orders, at less than one in thirty of the *adult* population; and some men would reckon them at more. They comprised, practically, all the modern classes which are most directly concerned with religion, literature and education; they answered roughly to our modern ministers of religion and schoolmasters, together with the large majority of scientists, authors and journalists. Everywhere, therefore, one met them in the way of business; and they were ubiquitous also as landlords. But to that subject I must come in the next chapter; for I have not yet said all that is absolutely necessary for the comprehension of Church influence in medieval society.

CHAPTER IV

Towns and Fields

THE town of the Middle Ages differed so little from the village that there is no sufficient reason for treating them separately when we are dealing with the all-important subject of ecclesiastical influence. The citizen, as well as the villager, knew the churchman as a great landlord. The wealth of the monks alone has sometimes been seriously estimated at one-third of the national wealth; we cannot put it into figures, but certainly it was enormous. This, naturally, had an immense effect upon social and economic life. Monks and bishops and other clerics owned serfs, just as they owned land; they, like the lay landlords, bought or sold serfs, or exchanged them for each other, or divided between them the brood of a bondman who was unlucky enough to belong to one lord while his wife was bondwoman to some other lord. We cannot blame the clerics for accepting the economic conditions of their own day, especially when we remember that the orthodox philosophy of that day expressly justified those conditions.

St Thomas Aquinas, the best representative of that philosophy, is like all his brethren in following Aristotle closely, almost slavishly, on most political or social questions. He agrees with Aristotle that what the Ideal State needs is a peasantry strong in the arm, dull of intellect, and divided from each other by mutual distrust. With regard to slavery and serfdom, again, he justifies them as not only an economically sound system, but morally defensible also. The heretic

Henry I's Nightmare
(from the Chronicle of John of Worcester)

Wyclif, so far as I know, was the only schoolman who refused to justify servitude in theory; and even he made no attempt to fight against it in practice. Therefore, when we face the facts as they undoubtedly were, we shall see that the enormous wealth of the Church was not likely to make for her popularity with the wage-earner. The monastic or episcopal landlord might be a few degrees easier than the squire; but there had been no parson-landlords in the days when Adam delved and Eve span. A little of the parish tithe might, in fact, go back to the poor of the parish, and a little more might go to beggars at the gate of that far-off monastery which took two-thirds of what the villagers had to pay; but such alms were too slight and too precarious to satisfy the full sense of justice.

Moreover, the whole system of Church dues was such as to generate a great deal of friction. Except tithes, all these offerings had originally been voluntary; it was only custom which had made them compulsory. The tithe, again, was a very heavy tax; it was practically an income tax of 2s. in the pound, extending downwards even to domestic servants, in so far as it was worth the collector's while to enforce it, and calculated on the gross income, without any allowance whatever for working expenses. From Exeter diocese, in 1287, we have an interesting example of this friction. The parson wanted his tithe of milk in the convenient form of cheese; but certain farmers declined to give it, except in the raw state. They brought it to church; and, if the priest were not there to receive it, then (as the bishop publicly complained) they poured it out on the ground before the altar, to the dishonour of God and Holy Church. Among the whole mass of medieval records, few subjects recur so frequently as tithe quarrels.

Finally, there was the *heriot* or *mortuary*, perhaps the most odious due of all. When a peasant died—that is, just at the moment when his family were at their

direst need—the serf's landlord might take his best
beast as a perquisite, and, in many cases, the priest his
next best, provided always that the family did not
possess less than three beasts in all. Therefore, in the
numerous cases where the monastery was both lord of
the manor and rector of the parish, a family which
owned only three cows would have to give up two at
the bread-winner's death. In towns, the best gown
was taken as a mortuary, or the brass cauldron, or the
bed on which the man had died.

A few cities apparently kept up their civic existence,
to a greater or less extent, even through the worst
barbarian invasions. In Britain, it is true, there is very
little evidence for a continuous survival of any city;
but there is far more in Italy, Spain, and France,
especially in the South. In those countries a certain
number seem to have kept their walls all through,
however dilapidated those walls may have been; and,
within those walls, there would naturally survive so
much of the old municipal traditions as would clearly
differentiate the in-dwellers from the villagers outside.
Yet, on the whole, we must look upon medieval city
life rather as a re-growth than as a survival of Roman
civilisation. It was, in fact, almost entirely a new
growth in the greater part of Germany, in Scandinavia
and the Low Countries and Britain, and in Northern
France. In all those districts the city was nearly always
a mere grown-up village. It generally owed its prosperity entirely to its favourable site. It stood by a
bridge, like Cambridge, or a ford, like Oxford and

Bedford, or an estuary, like King's Lynn, or at the gate of a castle, like Castle Rising, which sent two members to Parliament in my father's recollection. The peasants, in such lucky situations, prospered more than their neighbouring villagers; and, as time went on, they were able to buy privileges or liberties from their lord. For, of course, they had a lord, just like other villagers; he might be king or baron or squire or bishop or abbot, but he was at once their landlord and, to some real extent, master of their persons. The villagers, then, could now afford to buy privileges; and the wise lord would sell, since he would see that it was to his own interest to have a prosperous multitude on his estate, rather than a handful of starveling peasants. Moreover, he would sell also if he was sufficiently unwise, for then he would be in debt, and gaping for any offer of ready money. So the peasants gradually bought liberties and privileges with hard cash. Therefore, to the very end of the Middle Ages and even somewhat beyond, the municipal unit was to a great extent an agricultural unit also; the town was just a grown-up village. F. W. Maitland has written: "In the twelfth century, when William FitzStephen sings the praises of London, he does not say that somewhere near it lie fertile arable fields; he says that the arable fields of the town of London are fertile". At Cambridge, in 1279, when there were only 534 households in the whole town, 108 of these citizens possessed agricultural holdings; one had 58 acres, another 44; 21 possessed more than 10 acres each. There were 12 barns within the town itself. These, like some other medieval conditions, may be found more frequently surviving on the Continent than in England. Heidelberg, for instance, consists practically of two great streets running parallel with each other between the hillside and the river—the Hauptstrasse and the Plöck. In the middle of this latter street, at any rate nearly to the end of the nineteenth century, and possibly beyond, there survived a large farm-house with all its agricultural and pastoral appurtenances; horses and oxen in the stalls, and a dung-heap of gigantic size in the centre of the yard.

The houses in medieval towns, as in the villages, were nearly always of timber, except in districts where good stone was plentiful and wood was scarce. We may find cases where one is known by name as "*The Stone House*"; therefore, as a rule, the carpenter was far more in request than the mason for all buildings except churches and castles.

Cambridge owes its existence as a definite municipality to a charter of Henry I at the beginning of the twelfth century. In that charter the king (who was the lord here, for Cambridge, like Oxford, is a royal borough, a borough which grew up on the king's own estates) grants to his peasants the monopoly of river-trade in the district. No man, he decrees, shall load or unload boats, throughout the county, except at the royal wharf of Cambridge. How much the men paid for this particular monopoly we do not know. But we find one prosperous village buying its freedom from the

Bishop of Paris for a sum which would have the purchasing power of about £12,000 at the present moment; that, however, is an extreme case. With regard to Cambridge, we must note that the king sold to the villagers that which cost him nothing. It was at the expense of the rest of the county that Cambridge gained this monopoly of trade. At Leicester, on the other hand, about the same time, the citizens gained one of their chief liberties by what we should call nowadays a sporting chance, which determined them to buy, and their lord, the earl, to sell, the right of deciding their lawsuits by jury-trial, instead of by ordeal of battle. We know the details of this from a very interesting commission which reported in 1253 to the following effect:

The jurors say upon their oath that, in the days of Earl Robert [about 1120] two cousins, to wit Nicholas son of Aco and Geoffrey son of Nicholas, waged trial of battle for a certain plot of land which each claimed for his own; and they fought from sunrise even to noon and longer; and, as they thus fought, one of them drove the other to the verge of a little ditch; and, as he stood there on the verge and would have fallen in, his cousin said unto him "Take heed of the ditch behind thee, lest thou fall therein". Whereupon there arose so great a shouting and tumult from those who sat or stood around, that the lord Earl heard their clamour even in his castle, and asked then what it might be. And men answered him that two cousins were fighting for a plot of land, and one had driven the other to the ditch and had warned him when he stood on the brink and would have fallen therein. So the burgesses, moved then with pity, made a covenant with the lord Earl, that they should

THE LADDER OF SALVATION

Wall-Painting of about 1200 A.D. in Chaldon Church, Surrey

THE FIELDS OF CAMBRIDGE

From Loggan's engraving in 1688

FIFTEENTH-CENTURY STREET SCENE

TIMBER HOUSES IN PARIS

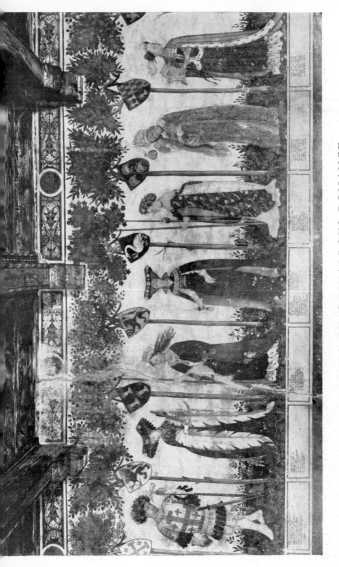

HEROINES OF CHIVALROUS ROMANCE

Fresco at the Castle of Manta in Piedmont

Ticommence li bures du granut Caam qui parole de la granut Tameine de perte
et de tartans et dinde Et des œurs merueille que aie munde sont.

THE POLOS EMBARKING AT VENICE

HOSPITAL IN THE FIFTEENTH CENTURY

(a) GRATIAN'S *DECRETUM*

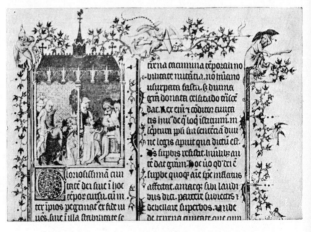

(b) ST AUGUSTINE'S *CITY OF GOD*

Specimens from two costly manuscripts

give him threepence yearly for each house which had a
gable on the High Street, on condition that he should grant
them [the right of judging their own pleas by a jury of
24 citizens], which right the lord Earl granted unto them.[1]

The citizens gained by this bargain, and the lord
gained still more definitely. In that way, step by step,
these communities bought the right of raising taxes in
their own way, so long as they paid a lump sum yearly
to the lord—this was called *Firma Burgi*, "the rent of
the borough." Again, they bought the right of paying
other dues directly, instead of through the sheriff; and
that of holding their own coroner's court, so long as
the king was not defrauded of his perquisites. For, in
nearly all medieval courts, the main question was that
of a fine to be paid by one party or the other, so that it
was a settled legal maxim: "Justice is a very profitable
job"—*Magnum emolumentum est justitia*.

Thus, before our period comes to an end, all the
English towns have obtained a great deal of self-
government. The most numerous and powerful, on
the whole, are on royal estates; and that for two
reasons. Our kings had bigger schemes than their
nobles, and therefore more need of money and a wider
outlook, and were therefore more ready to sell. Again,
when they delivered the goods, these were better
goods; the royal authority gave the citizens a better
guarantee, protected them more surely from the
encroachments of the sheriff or from the injustices of
any neighbouring baron, than a mere baron's or

[1] M. Bateson, *Records of the Borough of Leicester*, p. 41.

bishop's guarantee. Royal boroughs, therefore, were the luckiest; and the unluckiest were those whose lord was a bishop or an abbot. For these were necessarily conservative; to begin with, their property was not really their own: they were trustees for their successors, and therefore strictly forbidden by law to alienate their possessions. To this legal conservatism add the natural conservatism of a great churchman, and the fact that these ecclesiastical corporations, though not infrequently in debt, were seldom so hopelessly in arrears as baron or king; and you will understand why, as a matter of fact, one great chapter of municipal history in the Middle Ages is the struggle of the townsfolk against their ecclesiastical lord. At Lynn it was the bishop—for what is now King's Lynn was then Bishop's Lynn—at St Albans, Bury St Edmunds, and Burton it was the abbot.

CHAPTER V

Chivalry[1]

TACITUS, writing about 110 years after Christ, describes the Germanic peoples as transacting all their important business under arms. At the general assembly of the tribe, the "folk-moot", men signified approbation by clashing their weapons, and disapproval by a hollow murmur; in this way the final vote could be reckoned as unanimous, since the minority had gradually been intimidated into acquiescence.[2] Therefore the slave, who bore no arms, had no place in the folk-moot, nor had the boy who was yet unripe for war. When he was judged sufficient, he was solemnly and publicly invested with his future weapons; henceforward (writes Tacitus) "he belongs no longer to his family but to the state, and this 'Assumption of Arms'—*arma sumere*—is to the Germans what the assumption of the *toga virilis* is to us." Youthful aspirants would also attach themselves to some great warrior, living at his table and fighting in his battles, and

---

[1] For the purely military side of medieval knighthood see chapters xv, xviii and xix of my *Chaucer and his England*.

[2] Church councils, also, acted upon this theory of unanimity; the Vatican Council of 1870 is the first in all history in which it was formally resolved to decide by a mere majority vote. At Nicaea, minority bishops were punished till they yielded.

deeming themselves for ever disgraced if they escaped alive from a field on which their patron had fallen.

These ideas of chivalry were still further fortified by the example of the Arabs in Spain, who had independently evolved much the same ideal, and who, so far as can be traced, were definitely in advance even of the Troubadour civilisation of Southern France. In pride of race and valour, in minstrelsy of love and war, and even in courtesy towards their ladies, these Moors seem to have given more than they took from Spanish or Provençal society. The Church, again, took chivalry under her wing as she claimed to take all other human activities; and, though the purely secular ceremonies of knighthood survived all through the Middle Ages, yet there were also semi-ecclesiastical forms (including a nightly vigil by the altar and formal purificatory ablutions in the morning; hence our modern "Knights of the Bath") and, far more rarely, a purely ecclesiastical service in Latin, with the bishop as officiant (*Benedictio Novi Militis*).[1]

To the last, also, knighthood remained a close corporation; the knight must be chosen, not born. Serfs were sometimes admitted in earlier days, after proof of proportionate personal worth; but in later codes this was formally forbidden. Princes of the blood, on the other hand, claimed knighthood as of birth; but here again was the rare exception, at least until the end of the Middle Ages. The order was the blossom of a caste-system; it implied great privileges

[1] Both bath, and knighting on field, occur in Froissart.

and great responsibilities.[1] The poor were bound to respect the knight; but he was bound to defend the poor, and the helpless of all kinds. It is characteristic of the more primitive social conditions, even in Chaucer's day, that Langland reckons the knight's hunting activities, ideally, among his benefits to general society; for thus he destroyed the wild beasts which came from the forest to prey upon the village. On the other hand, we have explicit evidence of the hunters' occasional recklessness in riding over crops, and of the tenants' sufferings under game-preserving land-lords.[2]

In England, the decay of knighthood was due partly to the rise of the citizen class, partly to the Hundred Years' War and the Wars of the Roses. Already in the thirteenth century, statutes were passed compelling fairly well-to-do landed proprietors either to accept knighthood or to pay a fine in recognition of the duties and payments which they escaped by remaining untitled. In the fourteenth, the honour was conferred upon prominent London citizens like Walworth. In the Hundred Years' War, our armies were organised upon far truer business principles than those of our rivals; therefore we had far more promotion from the ranks; and among these self-made men were Sir Robert Knolles, who boasted that he was worth a

[1] Passages from contemporary authors, showing both sides of this ideal, and, on the other hand, comparing the practice with the ideal, may be found on pp. 281 ff. of my *Social Life in Britain*.
[2] E.g. Bishop of Chichester's rabbits in *Medieval Village*, p. 78.

king's ransom, and Sir John Hawkwood, who married an Italian princess with an enormous dowry. During the next century, many barons and their retainers exhausted themselves in the civil wars, so that feudalism had ceased to be a serious political force even before the Middle Ages were over. Almost the same may be said of France, though there the gain went to the kings rather than to the people. In Germany alone, of the great nations, the nobles and knights were a great political force even in the sixteenth century.

There are no books from which an unprofessional reader may learn so much of medieval chivalry, in a short compass, as from Joinville's memoirs of St Louis, and Froissart's chronicle. Joinville shows us his hero's natural and unaffected piety, his beauty of person, his courage in battle and his still more conspicuous firmness when he was a prisoner, and so wasted with dysentery that he could scarcely sit upright. We see him refusing to take to the boats in a shipwreck, lest the sailors should then abandon the vessel, and leave all the common folk to the mercy of the waves. Joinville is plainspoken about the king's hasty temper on certain occasions; but this lends all the more emphasis to his conspicuous sense of justice; under an oak in his park of Vincennes he was ready, on stated occasions, to hear the complaints of rich and poor. He inflicted an enormous fine on the Sire de Coucy, one of the greatest of his barons, for having hanged three boy-poachers of gentle birth. He was so far from taking advantage of our Henry III's domestic difficulties (as

Henry had taken advantage of his) that he granted him peace-terms which no other Frenchman, probably, would have granted. He had lived up to his own dying words to his son, "I had rather a Scotchman should come from Scotland and rule this kingdom justly, than that thou shouldst rule it ill".[1]

Froissart, writing at far greater length than Joinville, and with no such world-hero as St Louis in his foreground, gives us a picture with deeper shadows in contrast to his high lights. He speaks plainly of the ravage which accompanied Edward III's first campaign in Normandy, a country which had seen no serious war for a hundred years.[2]

When the king of England arrived in the Hogue Saint-Vaast, the king issued out of his ship, and the first foot that he set on the ground, he fell so rudely, that the blood brast out of his nose. The knights that were about him took him up and said: "Sir, for God's sake enter again into your ship, and come not aland this day, for this is but an evil sign for us". Then the king answered quickly and said: "Wherefore? This is a good token for me, for the land desireth to have me". Of the which answer all his men were right joyful. So that day and night the king lodged on the sands, and in the meantime discharged the ships of their horses and other baggages....

Thus they set forth as they were ordained, and they that

[1] Joinville's *Memoirs* are easily accessible in English (Everyman's Library).

[2] pp. 94 ff. All my page references to Froissart are to G. C. Macaulay's selections from Lord Berner's translation of 1523, a cheap and accessible volume which ought to be read by all who are interested in the real Middle Ages (Macmillan & Co., 1895).

went by the sea took all the ships that they found in their
ways: and so long they went forth, what by sea and what
by land, that they came to a good port and to a good town
called Barfleur, the which incontinent was won, for they
within gave up for fear of death. Howbeit, for all that, the
town was robbed, and much gold and silver there found,
and rich jewels: there was found so much riches, that the
boys and villains of the host set nothing by good furred
gowns: they made all the men of the town to issue out and
to go into the ships, because they would not suffer them to
be behind them for fear of rebelling again. After the town
of Barfleur was thus taken and robbed without brenning,
then they spread abroad in the country and did what they
list, for there was not to resist them. At last they came to a
great and a rich town called Cherbourg: the town they won
and robbed it, and brent part thereof, but into the castle
they could not come, it was so strong and well furnished
with men of war. Then they passed forth and came to
Montebourg, and took it and robbed and brent it clean.
In this manner they brent many other towns in that
country and won so much riches, that it was marvel to
reckon it. Then they came to a great town well closed
called Carentan, where there was also a strong castle and
many soldiers within to keep it. Then the lords came out
of their ships and fiercely made assault: the burgesses of
the town were in great fear of their lives, wives and
children: they suffered the Englishmen to enter into the
town against the will of all the soldiers that were there;
they put all their goods to the Englishmen's pleasures, they
thought that most advantage. When the soldiers within
saw that, they went into the castle: the Englishmen went
into the town, and two days together they made sore
assaults, so that when they within saw no succour, they
yielded up, their lives and goods saved, and so departed.

The Englishmen had their pleasure of that good town and castle, and when they saw they might not maintain to keep it, they set fire therein and brent it, and made the burgesses of the town to enter into their ships, as they had done with them of Barfleur, Cherbourg and Montebourg, and of other towns that they had won on the sea-side....It was no marvel though they of the country were afraid, for before that time they had never seen men of war, nor they wist not what war or battle meant. They fled away as far as they might hear speaking of the Englishmen, and left their houses well stuffed, and granges full of corn, they wist not how to save and keep it. The king of England and the prince had in their battle a three thousand men of arms and six thousand archers and a ten thousand men afoot, besides them that rode with the marshals.

Thus as ye have heard, the king rode forth, wasting and brenning the country without breaking of his order. He left the city of Coutances and went to a great town called Saint-Lô, a rich town of drapery and many rich burgesses. In that town there were dwelling an eight or nine score burgesses, crafty men. When the king came there, he took his lodging without, for he would never lodge in the town for fear of fire: but he sent his men before and anon the town was taken and clean robbed. It was hard to think the great riches that there was won, in clothes specially; cloth would there have been sold good cheap, if there had been any buyers.

Take, again, one of Froissart's many business-like references to the profits made by successful soldiers from their prisoners' ransoms (p. 349). He is describing the battle of Aljubarrota in Portugal (1385), where the English and Portuguese defeated the Spaniards and French. After the first victorious shock, the English and their allies found heavy reinforcements coming against them; and then,

As soon as they had discomfited the vaward and had taken their prisoners, and that they saw none other battle coming within their sight, yet for all that they would put no trust in their first victory: therefore they sent six notable persons to go and aview the country, to see if they should have any more to do. They that rode forth came and saw the king of Castile's great battle coming to them-ward fast approaching to Juberoth, more than twenty thousand horsemen. Then they returned as fast as they might and said all on high to the people: "Sirs, advise you well, for as yet we have done nothing: behold yonder cometh the king of Castile with his great battle with more than twenty thousand men, there is none tarried behind". When they heard those tidings, they took short counsel, which was of necessity: then incontinent they ordained a piteous deed, for every man was commanded on pain of death to slay their prisoners without mercy, noble, gentle, rich nor other, none except. Then the lords, knights and squires that were prisoners were in a hard case, for there was no prayer that availed them from the death; and so they were slain, some in one place and some in another, as they were spread abroad unarmed weening to have been saved, but they were not. To say truth it was great pity, for every man slew his prisoner, and he that did not, other men slew them in their hands; and the Portugalois and the English-men who had given that counsel said it was better to slay than to be slain: "For if we kill them not, while we be a fighting they will escape and slay us, for there is no trust in a man's enemy". Thus was slain by great mischief the lord of Lignac, sir Peter of Quer, the lord of l'Espres, the lord of Bernecque, the lord of Bordes, sir Bertrand of Bareges, the lord of Morianne, sir Raymond d'Arzac, sir John of

Assolegie, sir Monaut of Saramen, sir Peter of Salebiere,
sir Stephen Valencin, sir Stephen Corasse, sir Peter Have-
fane, and to the number of three hundred squires of Bearn;
and of France sir John of Rye, sir Geoffrey Richon, sir
Geoffrey Partenay and divers other. Lo, behold the great
evil adventure that fell that Saturday, for they slew as many
good prisoners as would well have been worth, one with
another, four hundred thousand franks.

He shows us plenty of bright pageantry; the most
elaborate is his description of the welcome, in 1389, to
Isabel of Bavaria, the new queen of France, of whom
it was said afterwards that she had played Eve to the
Virgin Mary of Joan of Arc: that Isabel had ruined
France, as the Maid had saved it.

There was such people in the streets [writes Froissart,
p. 383], that it seemed that all the world had been there.
At the first gate of Saint Denis entering into Paris there was
a heaven made full of stars, and within it young children
apparelled like angels sweetly singing, and among them an
image of our Lady holding in figure her little child playing
by himself with a little mill made of a great nut: this
heaven was high and richly apparelled with the arms of
France, with a banner of the sun shining of gold, casting
his rays; the which was the device of the king for the
feast of the jousts. The queen and the other ladies, as they
passed under in at the gate, they had great pleasure to
behold it, and so had all other that passed by. Then when
the queen and the ladies were passed by, then they came a
soft pace before the fountain in the street of Saint Denis,
which conduit was covered over with a cloth of fine azure
painted full of flower-de-luces of gold, and the pillars were
set full of the arms of divers noble lords of France; and out
of this fountain there issued in great streams piment,

[spiced wine] and claret, and about this fountain there were young maidens richly apparelled, with rich chaplets on their heads, singing melodiously; great pleasure it was to hear them, and they held in their hands cups and goblets of gold, offering and giving to drink all such as passed by; and the queen rested there and regarded them and had great pleasure of that device, and so did all other ladies and damosels that saw it....And all the street of Saint Denis was covered over with cloths of silk and camlet, such plenty as though such cloths should cost nothing. And I, sir John Froissart, author of this history, was present and saw all this and had great marvel where such number of cloths of silk were gotten; there was as great plenty as though they had been in Alisandre or Damas: and all the houses on both sides of the great street of Saint Denis unto the bridge of Paris were hanged with cloths of Arras of divers histories, the which was pleasure to behold....

Then they passed forth and came to the bridge of Paris, which was covered and richly beseen, the covering of green and crimson full of stars and the streets hanged, to Our Lady's church. And by that time that the queen and the ladies were past the bridge and approached to the church of Our Lady, it was late, for all the way as they went they rode but a soft pace; and or the queen and the ladies entered into the church of Our Lady, they found by their way other plays and pastimes greatly to their pleasure. Among all other there was a master came out of Genoa; he had tied a cord on the highest house on the bridge of Saint Michael over all the houses, and the other end was tied on the highest tower in Our Lady's church; and as the queen passed by, and was in the great street called Our Lady's street, because it was late this said master with two brenning candles in his hands issued out of a little stage that he had made on the height of Our Lady's tower, and

66

singing he went upon the cord all along the great street, so
that that saw him had marvel how it might be, and he
bare still in his hands two brenning candles, so that it
might well be seen all over Paris and two mile without
Paris: he was such a tumbler that his lightness was greatly
praised.

Yet all this is scarcely half of the festivities which
Froissart describes on that day.

He shows us the contrasts that come out so glaringly
in medieval society; most striking of all, perhaps, is
that of the Black Prince after his two victories of
Poitiers and of Limoges. At Poitiers (p. 130):

It was nigh night or all came from the chase. And as it
was reported, there was slain all the flower of France, and
there was taken with the king and the lord Philip his son
a seventeen earls, beside barons, knights and squires, and
slain a five or six thousand of one and other. When every
man was come from the chase, they had twice as many
prisoners as they were in number in all. Then it was
counselled among them because of the great charge and
doubt to keep so many, that they should put many of them
to ransom incontinent in the field, and so they did: and
the prisoners found the Englishmen and Gascons right
courteous; there were many that day put to ransom and let
go all only on their promise of faith and truth to return
again between that and Christmas to Bordeaux with their
ransoms. Then that night they lay in the field beside
whereas the battle had been: some unarmed them, but not
all, and unarmed all their prisoners, and every man made
good cheer to his prisoner.... When sir James Audley was
brought to his lodging, then he sent for sir Peter Audley his
brother and for the lord Bartholomew of Burghersh, the
lord Stephen of Cosington, the lord of Willoughby and the

lord Ralph Ferrers, all these were of his lineage, and then he called before him his four squires, that had served him that day well and truly. Then he said to the said lords: "Sirs, it hath pleased my lord the prince to give me five hundred marks of revenues by year in heritage, for the which gift I have done him but small service with my body. Sirs, behold here these four squires, who hath always served me truly and specially this day: that honour that I have is by their valiantness. Wherefore I will reward them: I give and resign into their hands the gift that my lord the prince hath given me of five hundred marks of yearly revenues, to them and to their heirs for ever, in like manner as it was given me. I clearly disherit me thereof and inherit them without any repeal or condition". The lords and other that were there, every man beheld other and said among themselves: "It cometh of a great nobleness to give this gift". They answered him with one voice: "Sir, be it as God will; we shall bear witness in this behalf wheresoever we be come"....

The same day of the battle at night the prince made a supper in his lodging to the French king and to the most part of the great lords that were prisoners....

And always the prince served before the king as humbly as he could, and would not sit at the king's board for any desire that the king could make, but he said he was not sufficient to sit at the table with so great a prince as the king was. But then he said to the king: "Sir, for God's sake make none evil nor heavy cheer, though God this day did not consent to follow your will; for, sir, surely the king my father shall bear you as much honour and amity as he may do, and shall accord with you so reasonably that ye shall ever be friends together after. And, sir, methink ye ought to rejoice, though the journey be not as ye would have had it, for this day ye have won the high renown of prowess

68

and have passed this day in valiantness all other of your party. Sir, I say not this to mock you, for all that be on our party, that saw every man's deeds, are plainly accorded by true sentence to give you the prize and chaplet". Therewith the Frenchmen began to murmur and said among themselves how the prince had spoken nobly, and that by all estimation he should prove a noble man, if God send him life and to persevere in such good fortune.

At Limoges, the Prince was already sick of his mortal sickness, and was incensed by the fact that the city had been betrayed to the French. When he retook it (p. 201):

Then the prince, the duke of Lancaster, the earl of Cambridge, the earl of Pembroke, sir Guichard d'Angle and all the other with their companies entered into the city, and all other foot-men, ready apparelled to do evil, and to pill and rob the city, and to slay men, women and children, for so it was commanded them to do. It was great pity to see the men, women and children that kneeled down on their knees before the prince for mercy; but he was so inflamed with ire, that he took no heed to them, so that none was heard, but all put to death, as they were met withal, and such as were nothing culpable. There was no pity taken of the poor people, who wrought never no manner of treason, yet they bought it dearer than the great personages, such as had done the evil and trespass. There was not so hard a heart within the city of Limoges, an if he had any remembrance of God, but that wept piteously for the great mischief that they saw before their eyen: for more than three thousand men, women and children were slain and beheaded that day. God have mercy on their souls, for I trow they were martyrs....

Now let us speak of the knights that were within the

city, as sir John of Villemur, sir Hugh de la Roche, Roger Beaufort, son to the earl of Beaufort, captains of the city. When they saw the tribulation and pestilence that ran over them and their company, they said to one another: "We are all dead, without we defend ourselves: therefore let us sell our lives dearly, as good knights ought to do". Then sir John of Villemur said to Roger Beaufort: "Roger, it behoveth that ye be made a knight". Then Roger answered and said: "Sir, I am not as yet worthy to be a knight: I thank you, sir, of your good-will". So there was no more said: they had not the leisure to speak long together. Howbeit, they assembled them together in a place against an old wall and there displayed their banners. So they were to the number of eighty persons. Thither came the duke of Lancaster, the earl of Cambridge and their companies and so lighted afoot, so that the Frenchmen could not long endure against the Englishmen, for anon they were slain and taken. Howbeit, the duke of Lancaster himself fought long hand to hand against sir John Villemur, who was a strong knight and a hardy, and the earl of Cambridge fought against sir Hugh de la Roche, and the earl of Pembroke against Roger Beaufort, who was as then but a squire. These three Frenchmen did many feats of arms: their men were occupied otherwise. The prince in his chariot came by them and beheld them gladly and appeased himself in beholding of them. So long they fought together that the three Frenchmen, by one accord holding out their swords, said: "Sirs, we be yours, ye have conquered us: do with us according to right of arms". "Sir", quoth the duke of Lancaster, "we look for nothing else: therefore we receive you as our prisoners". And thus the foresaid three Frenchmen were taken, as it was informed me.

Thus the city of Limoges was pilled, robbed and clean

brent and brought to destruction. Then the Englishmen departed with their conquest and prisoners and drew to Cognac, where my lady the princess was. Then the prince gave leave to all his men of war to depart and did no more that season; for he felt himself not well at ease, for always his sickness increased, whereof his brethren and people were sore dismayed.

Finally, let us hear Froissart's epitaph on an honourable knight and a great general, Sir John Chandos, whose prowess had saved Guienne for the English crown. In 1369, there was a chance encounter at the bridge of Lussac, where the English, being outnumbered, had the worst to begin with, but were presently reinforced and, now with superior numbers, gained a considerable victory. The English general had fallen first of all in that fight (p. 197).

Sir John Chandos, who was a right hardy and a courageous knight, with his banner before him and his company about him, with his coat of arms on him great and large, beaten with his arms of white sarcenet and two piles gules one before and another behind, so that he seemed to be a sufficient knight to do a great feat of arms, and as one of the foremost with his glaive in his hand marched to his enemies. The same morning there had fallen a great dew, so that the ground was somewhat moist, and so in his going forward he slode and fell down at the joining with his enemies; and as he was arising there lit a stroke on him given by a squire called Jaques of Saint-Martin with his glaive, the which stroke entered into the flesh under his eye between the nose and the forehead. Sir John Chandos saw not the stroke coming on that side, for he was blind on the one eye. He lost the sight thereof a five year before, as

71

he hunted after an hart in the launds of Bordeaux, and also he had on no visor. The stroke was rude and entered into his brain, the which stroke grieved him so sore, that he overthrew to the earth and turned for pain two times up-se-down, as he that was wounded to death; for after the stroke he never spake word. And when his men saw that misfortune, they were right dolorous: then his uncle Edward Clifford stept and bestrode him, for the Frenchmen would fain have had him, and defended him so valiantly and gave round about him such strokes, that none durst approach near to him: also sir John Clanvowe and sir Bertram of Casselis seemed like men out of their minds, when they saw their master lie on the earth.

Then, when the whole fight was over,

The barons and knights of Poitou were sore discomforted, when they saw their seneschal sir John Chandos lie on the earth and could not speak. Then they lamentably complained and said, "Ah, sir John Chandos, the flower of all chivalry, unhappily was that glaive forged that thus hath wounded you and brought you in peril of death". They wept piteously that were about him, and he heard and understood them well, but he could speak no word. They wrung their hands and tare their hairs and made many a pitiful complaint, and specially such as were of his own house. Then his servants unarmed him and laid him on pavises and so bare him softly to Mortimer, the next fortress to them. And the other barons and knights returned to Poitiers and led with them their prisoners: and as I understood, the same Jaques Martin that thus hurt sir John Chandos was so little taken heed to of his hurts, that he died at Poitiers. And this noble knight sir John Chandos lived not after his hurt past a day and a night, but so died. God have mercy on his soul: for a hundred year past there had not been a more courteous nor more fuller of noble virtues and good conditions among the Englishmen than he was....For his death his friends and also some of his enemies were right sorrowful. The Englishmen loved him, because all nobleness was found in him: the Frenchmen hated him because they redoubted him: yet I heard his death greatly complained among right noble and valiant knights of France, saying that it was a great damage of his death, for they said: "Better it had been that he had been taken alive; for if he had been taken alive", they said, "he was so sage and so imaginative, that he would have found some manner of good means whereby the peace might have ensued between the realms of England and France: for he was so well beloved with the king of England, that the king would believe him rather than any other in the world".

CHAPTER VI

Monasticism

FROM the castle let us turn to the abbey. Monasticism grew up naturally and sometimes independently in different districts; indeed, it is to some real extent a pre-Christian institution. In the Eastern Church, from very early times, men began to go out from Alexandria and other great cities into the deserts of Egypt and Syria; and the movement was intensified when Constantine made Christianity into the State Church. Religious enthusiasts, as Harnack puts it, "fled from the world, and therefore from a Church which had admitted the world to her bosom". Not, of course, that the movement was in any sense anticlerical; but simply that the anchorite found himself more or less independent of the priest, and set himself to work out his own salvation. In process of time these anchorites formed groups; then larger groups; then the necessity of legislation was felt, and some leader drew up a formal rule, which all undertook to obey. The earliest of these rules was that of Pachomius, but in the East the greatest and most popular was that of St Basil, who died in 379.

In the West, by far the most influential rule was that of St Benedict, drawn up probably in A.D. 529. Even the widest spread and best known of Western monks, when they were called by other names, were either simply reformed Benedictines (such were the Cluniacs and the Cistercians) or at least, like the Carthusians, owed much to his example. The next most numerous monastic clergy, for many centuries, were the Canons Regular, all of whom followed, in slightly different forms, a rule of life which was believed to have been drawn up by St Augustine; hence the name *Augustinian* (or *Austin*) *Canons*. In the early thirteenth century, the friars came forward; the Franciscans in almost explicit revolt from certain Benedictine usages and tendencies, and the Dominicans as a sort of reformed Canons Regular; the Carmelites and Austin friars, though claiming earlier and independent origin, were really constituted in imitation of these their predecessors. Each of these Orders, with very few exceptions, had a corresponding Order of nuns; and, though many who had taken the vows were not clerics in the strictest sense, yet all enjoyed full ecclesiastical immunities; and these votaries formed the *Regular Clergy*, each bound by his own *Regula*, or Rule, as distinguished from the *Secular Clergy*, who lived in the world (*in saeculo*) as prelates, canons of great churches, parish priests, parish clerks, unattached clerics doing all those kinds of work which are connected nowadays with the designation "clerk" and the frequently-used adjective "clerical".

The Benedictine may be taken as typical of all the older Orders. He took a lifelong vow to keep the "Three Substantials"—Obedience, Poverty, and Chastity. From these three essentials not even the Pope could absolve him; the Pope could indeed so far annul the whole vow as to make a monk into a non-monk (though actual examples are extremely rare); but no papal dispensation could excuse from mortal sin the monk who broke any one of the three substantials. These were supported on four main pillars; the Rule commanded absence of all private property, total abstinence from butcher's meat except in case of sickness, steady manual labour, and strict confinement within the monastic precincts. About four-and-a-half hours of the day were allotted to public psalmody and prayer, apart from voluntary private devotions; these services gradually grew more elaborate; in 1500 the really strict monk spent some six hours of his day in church. St Benedict recommended also some three or four hours of daily reading in devotional books; but he made definite allowance for illiterate monks. The Rule is a model of practical and spiritual wisdom combined; it has been called the greatest document of the whole Middle Ages. It had much influence on the evolution of the Canons Regular, whom modern authors often separate from the monks with a certain pedantic exaggeration; though in the Middle Ages both classes were sometimes included under the one term, and even the most pedantic accuracy allows us to apply *monastic*, *monastery*, to Canons Regular and friars as well as to monks. The Canons Regular were less strictly cut off from meat than the Benedictines, and less strictly enclosed; it was common, in fact, for them to serve as parish priests in their own appropriated churches.

The friars reacted consciously and deliberately, on certain important points, against the older Orders. The monk was "possessionate"; however strictly he, personally, might abdicate all private property, his monastery was endowed, and often with enormous wealth. The friar, on the other hand, was theoretically a complete mendicant, and was in fact very slenderly endowed in comparison with the possessionates. Again, the monk was cloistered strictly, and even the Canon Regular to some extent; but for the friars, the monastery was only a base of operations; they wandered forth from it, by twos and twos, to beg and preach and hear confessions in the parishes; this, of course, involved not infrequent competition with the parish priest, and sometimes severe friction. Monks and nuns could seldom be really democratic in their sympathies; a very small proportion of them were recruited from the poorer classes; the nuns, indeed, hardly ever, since a nunnery soon came to be regarded as the natural destination of well-born girls whose parents could not provide them with marriage-portions commensurate with their rank; it is quite possible that Chaucer's Prioress was even better-born than his Knight. Friars, on the other hand, after the first fervour of the movement had cooled down, were far more often from the wage-earning masses, far more in touch with all classes, and far more dependent upon popular support. They were sometimes accused (as, on the other hand, the

Lollards were) of preaching levelling doctrines and thus contributing to the Peasants' Revolt of 1381.

Monasticism, it will thus be seen, was a growth perfectly natural to the unsettled world of the Dark Ages, where it seemed too hard in most cases to follow Christ truly, and to work out one's own salvation effectually, without retiring into the wilderness. During the more orderly, but still unquiet, centuries of the Middle Ages proper, it was still doing work which could scarcely have been done otherwise in such a society as it had to face. Even at the Reformation, the average cloisterer was living a more decent life than the average outsider; but this standard was no longer sufficiently high to defend his wealth and his privileges successfully. Partly, no doubt, this was because he himself had contributed to raise the standard of outside society; but the main causes of the Dissolution lay in the undeniable decay—it may be even said, in the avowed abandonment—of the early monastic ideal. This transpires, not only from the accusations of their enemies, not only from the plain confessions of their own friends, but still more clearly from the formal monastic records: account-rolls, reports of episcopal visitors, and proceedings of the Benedictine, Augustinian, or Mendicant General Chapters.

Let us take in order those four prescriptions which I have called the four main pillars.

(1) The prohibition of private property had broken down altogether. Twice, just before and just after

1200, popes had decreed that the monk found in possession of private property at his death should be buried in the dunghill, in token of his damnation; yet, during all the later generations of the Middle Ages, cloisterers were not only receiving illegal pocket-money under different excuses, but this irregularity had become so regular and notorious that, whenever a parsimonious or impecunious superior refused it, the sufferers actually appealed against him to the official visitor, who never gave them the plain answer that they were demanding an illegal thing.

(2) The prohibition of butcher's meat had become equally unreal. Gradually, monks had formed the habit of going to the infirmary, where flesh was allowed, and eating it there. Popes and disciplinarians naturally fulminated against this abuse, but in vain. In many cases, indeed, the legal fiction took another form; a chamber was built midway between refectory and infirmary, in which the monks might eat flesh, while still banishing it from the refectory. Such a chamber was generally called "misericord", the Room of Mercy. In 1236 this practice was forbidden by St Francis's friend Gregory IX, a pope greatly concerned for monastic reform. But neither his prohibition nor that of other disciplinarians was of real avail; and when, in 1337, Benedict XII set himself even more earnestly than Gregory IX to the task of monastic reform, he was obliged to make terms with the abuse. The misericord system was permitted, so long as only half the community used the room at any given time; thus the

monks might now legally eat flesh on alternate days. But, granted this inch, they took an ell; and we find, shortly afterwards, even the English Benedictine Chapter complaining that the prohibition on alternate days is too strict for "modern" monks, who are no longer capable of the self-denial which characterised their forefathers.

(3) Labour was abandoned earlier still, and more completely. St Maur, who had been St Benedict's pupil, is recorded to have said that, since by this time the monasteries are all well endowed, it is no longer necessary for the monks to work as labourers. Certainly that soon became the general view; and, although each successive monastic reformer attempted to revive the old rule of manual labour, this revival scarcely ever lasted more than a generation or two. Before 1300, it had become very exceptional for monks to work with their own hands in the fields or at any handicraft. The services they rendered to agriculture were rather as landlords than as labourers; and even as landlords, in the later Middle Ages, there was little to choose between the monks and the laymen. The account-rolls tell us that monks did not even shave themselves, wash their own linen, do their own kitchen or household work, or mow their own cloister-garth; these things were done by hired servants, male or female. In a large monastery, there were usually servants in the proportion of three to every two monks.

(4) Claustration, again, had become a dead letter. Very early in monastic history, the multiplicity of

estates, houses and privileges compelled the officials—
sacristan, cellarer, almoner, granator, etc.—to become
active business men, constantly abroad on what, after
all, were fundamentally worldly affairs. An abbot of
about A.D. 1200, Philippe de Harvengt, complains that
monks are ubiquitous on all the roads, in all the
markets, and at every fair. Later visitational records
show that there was scarcely any attempt to appeal to
the rule of strict claustration, and that Chaucer's
Shipman's Tale, where the monk of St Denis comes out
whenever he likes to visit his friends in Paris, is a
perfectly natural picture of ordinary practice. Indeed,
matters went so far that the Rule was enforced on this
point only as a very exceptional punishment. The
English General Chapter of 1444 decreed three weeks
of confinement to the precincts for any monk who calls
his brother a liar, *mentiris*, and a whole year for one
who strikes his fellow-monk deliberately with fist or
knife. As a present-day parallel to this, we might
imagine an authoritative decree in the United States
to the effect that similar periods of actual abstention
from whisky, as apart from nominal abstention, should
be inflicted on citizens guilty of similar slanders or
assaults.

The same decline from earlier ideals may be traced
in every department of religious life. The account-rolls
show that not one-tenth of the enormous monastic
incomes were spent upon charitable purposes; and
frequently the monks were not even giving to the poor
all the money which had been definitely earmarked for

them by the donors, and of which the monasteries, therefore, were not owners but simply trustees. It is equally evident that, in a good many cases, they were no longer familiar even with the Latin of their service-books. To that revival of learning which bore its best fruit in the creation of the Universities, from about 1175 onwards, the older and religious Orders contributed very little; scarcely any monk or Canon Regular, out of all those thousands, distinguished himself as a University teacher; and though Benedict XII attempted to raise the standard of learning by decreeing that a certain proportion should be sent to study at the Universities, that proportion was not really kept. The friars, it is true, did contribute very much to University life, and produced the most distinguished among the scholastic philosophers; but their energy in this direction was spent before the Reformation; in 1500, they were mainly a conservative or reactionary force. There is overwhelming evidence for a general feeling that the monastic Orders were no longer justifying their enormous endowments and their exceptional privileges, which rendered them almost a state within the State.[1] The strongest condemnation came sometimes from the ablest and most orthodox writers; moreover, even when an apologist writes most voluminously and most energetically against the attacks of Lollards and other heretics, it will always be

[1] I have printed, in the second volume of my *Five Centuries of Religion* (cc. 26–28), the generalisations of some 120 contemporary witnesses. Nearly all of these are strikingly unfavourable, even when all allowance has been made for medieval exaggeration of language.

found that, when he comes to the monastic question, he either shirks it as much as possible or adopts a far less confident tone. The facts have been summed up in our own day by a perfectly orthodox Roman Catholic historian in France: "Medieval literature, whether rightly or wrongly, does censure monastic morals in crude terms and without distinction".[1]

By far the most valuable series of original monastic documents, accessible to the general reader, are the episcopal visitations of Lincoln diocese in the mid-fifteenth century, edited and translated for the Lincoln Record Society, in three volumes, by Professor A. Hamilton Thompson. To the student, almost equally valuable are the four volumes published in the Camden Society series, *Visitations of the Diocese of Norwich* and *Collectanea Anglo-Premonstratensia*; but these were not well edited, and have not been translated. The seven volumes cover practically the whole century preceding the Reformation in England; and they show clearly why the candid Roman Catholic Lingard, when accused by a friend of having abandoned the monks' cause too easily in his *History of England*, wrote that frank letter which is still in the records of Ushaw College, to explain that any modern attempt to whitewash the institution, as it was under Henry VIII, must in the long run prove disastrous.[2] However indefensible

[1] G. Mollat, *Les Papes d'Avignon*, 1912, p. 234.

[2] I have printed the words in full on p. 458 of my *Five Centuries of Religion*, II. Compare Lingard's words (in his *Life* by Haile & Bonney, p. 184) to a fellow-Roman Catholic who had asked why he said that all the monks had submitted to Henry VIII's supremacy: "If I must

many of Henry's methods were, and however little we may trust the reports of the hasty visits which he instituted for his own political purpose, the careful episcopal visitations of that last medieval century tell very much the same tale. Not all monks were the same, of course; but the institution, as a whole, no longer deserved its exceptional place as a vast world-force in society. Five of the largest monasteries of which we have abundant record—St Albans, Norwich, Peterborough, Ramsey and Walsingham—were certainly in a bad state; and for others, such as Westminster, there are ominous indications, quite apart from all that is recorded against many smaller houses. Perhaps St Albans was the worst; but of Peterborough and Ramsey we have fuller details, thanks to the bishops of Lincoln. At Peterborough we have the inner history of thirteen consecutive years; it is a monotonous record of waste, indiscipline, and neglect even of the daily Church services.[1] In the last report, the abbot's adulteries with three separate women are reported as matters of common notoriety; and though the visiting bishop formally exonerated him, by the cheap process of exculpation known as *compurgation*, yet at the same time he punished two of the women; a significant contrast. At Ramsey, the services were as shamefully

disclose the reason—he will perhaps approve of my silence in the history—I will answer with Cardinal Pole, that the monks of that period were men of little reputation and had entirely (*prorsus*) degenerated from the spirit of their original institute....They were a degenerate, time-serving class of men".

[1] I have summed this up briefly in *History* for Jan. 1930.

neglected as at Peterborough. Taking, as a whole, the seventy different visitations recorded for monasteries in Lincoln diocese during the fifteenth century,[1] we find that in forty-five cases the monks or nuns were violating one of the most elementary and necessary by-laws—that the accounts of the house should be kept in writing and duly audited. In some cases, there is evidence that this neglect had been going on for years, and the monastery was deep in debt, while the buildings fell into decay. Again, a strict by-law forbade sitting up to drink after compline, the last service of the day; yet at twenty-six monasteries this habit of forbidden potations is recorded, and sometimes with the additional complaint that the monks are thus rendered incapable of rising to perform the night services. Masses were often neglected, to the fraud of benefactors' souls. Almsgiving was curtailed in twenty-three of the houses, often with very gross embezzlement of the funds earmarked for charity, and the rules of claustration and vegetarianism had become almost a dead letter. Some of the monks could not even read the Latin in which their service-books were written.

When, therefore, political interests and greed for money conspired in suggesting to Henry VIII that he should attack the monasteries, he had no real difficulty in suppressing them; the public knew what Cardinal Pole confessed later on, that the monks had degene-

[1] Published in Latin and English by Professor A. Hamilton Thompson (Lincoln Record Society, 1914, 1918, 1929).

rated from the early spirit of their institution. The great rebellion in the North, the "Pilgrimage of Grace", was far from being purely pro-monastic; yet the North, where civilisation was most backward and where people were far more dependent on monastic help than in the South, was the only part of England where there were serious troubles. The king was able to bring the citizen-levies of the South against the rebels; and, though the transference of many monastic estates to mere courtiers and upstarts did unquestionably accentuate the economic crisis of the sixteenth century, yet time justified the principle (though not by any means all the methods) of Henry's policy. In the first place, even Mary found herself obliged to accept the Dissolution as an accomplished fact. Secondly, those countries of Europe which kept their monasteries untouched by the Reformation have all, sooner or later, suppressed them, and only allowed them, as in England, to grow up again as best they could with fresh endowments.[1] Thirdly, however the poor may have lost temporarily through the Dissolution—and their losses have often been exaggerated to an absurd extent, in defiance of plain documentary evidence— yet the British poor, on the whole, have been far better off since the Reformation than their fellows in countries which kept their monasteries, such as France and Italy

---

[1] This revival, of course, bears testimony to the value of the monastic ideal for a certain number of people; but it is still far from justifying the enormous numerical and economic preponderance of the monks in the sixteenth century.

and Spain. It is doubtful whether they were not better off at their very worst, during that past troubled generation of religious and social revolution; and certainly the British peasants and poorer artisans were far less miserable than the corresponding classes of France under the *Ancien Régime*.

CHAPTER VII

Trade and Travel

ONE of the most important factors in medieval civic life was the Gild. Such corporations are in one sense prehistoric; they represent the instinct of combination for self-preservation which we see even in animals. But, to a considerable extent, also, they represent a conscious effort, conscious constitution-making. It was not only that the citizens said, "We will form a gild", but the lord might say also, "You shall form a gild". In the most important of these, the gild merchant, both forces can clearly be traced. In many towns the gild merchant consisted of all full freemen; in all towns where it existed it represented the main power of the freemen. As town life developed, the Craft Gilds grew up; the tailors' trade union, the saddlers' trade union, and so on. Finally, the most numerous of all were the religious gilds, some very small but others quite large and powerful, in which the members clubbed together to earn in common certain spiritual benefits and to help their own sick or poor. Thus they were the medieval benefit societies; and their suppression at the Reformation, on the excuse of superstition, was a very great injustice.

The gild system was useful for the time; but those who sometimes hold it up as a model for our own time have not, I think, fully faced the facts. A Cambridge student, who has for some years been looking closely into the evidence for the actual working of those gilds, confirms my conviction that it is extraordinarily misleading to argue from the theory of the medieval gild to its actual practice. Even in theory the gild was often merciless to rival organisations, or to the community at large. At Derby, for instance, in 1330, it was testified before a Royal Commission that the merchant gild tyrannised over the other townsfolk. They report that when wool or leather or hides are brought into the town for sale, if a member of the gild sets his foot upon the article, and offers a price for it, then nobody outside the gild will dare to buy it, nor will the owner dare to sell it except to a gild-man, nor at a higher price than he offers. "The profit arising therefrom", they add, "does not accrue to the advantage of the borough, but only to the advantage of those who are of the said gild." And again: "such usages redound to the injury, oppression, and pauperisation of the people".

There you have the seamy side, as against what the gild system sometimes did for good in the way of helping the town to buy a cargo of corn or coal wholesale, and to distribute it among the community at reasonable prices, like our rationing system during the War. Again, the gilds did undoubted good in keeping up the standard of workmanship and in fighting against adulteration. Yet in neither of those aims were they entirely successful. Even as early as

the days of Chaucer's great-grandfather, men sometimes complained, almost as they complain nowadays,
that you cannot get a genuine article in the shops, any
more than you can get a good servant, or find a child
who has been sufficiently disciplined with the rod.
Berthold of Regensburg (about 1250) recurs more than
once to this subject in his famous sermons; let me give
here a few sentences from the long rehearsal of tricks
in every craft and trade which I have translated fully
in my *Life in the Middle Ages* (III, 57).

The first [tricksters] are ye that work in clothing, silks,
or wool or fur, shoes or gloves or girdles. Men can in no
wise dispense with you; men must needs have clothing,
therefore should ye so serve them as to do your work truly;
not to steal half the cloth, or to use other guile; mixing hair
with your wool or stretching it out longer, whereby a man
thinketh to have gotten good cloth, yet thou hast stretched
it to be longer than it should be, and makest a good cloth
into useless stuff. Nowadays no man can find a good hat
for thy falsehood; the rain will pour 'down through the
brim into his bosom. Even such deceit is there in shoes, in
furs, in currier's work; one man sells an old skin for a new,
and how manifold are your deceits no man knoweth so
well as thou and thy master the devil.... The second folk
are all such as work with iron tools.... Such should all be
true and trustworthy in their office, whether they work by
the day or by the piece, as many carpenters and masons do.
When they labour by the day, they should not stand all the
more idle that they may multiply the days at their work.
If thou labourest by the piece, then thou shouldest not
hasten too soon therefrom, that thou mayest be rid of the
work as quickly as possible, and that the house may fall

down in a year or two; thou shouldest work at it truly, even as it were thine own. Thou smith, thou wilt shoe a steed with a shoe that is naught; and the beast will go perchance scarce a mile thereon when it is already broken, and the horse may go lame, or a man be taken prisoner or lose his life. Thou art a devil and an apostate; thou must go to the apostate angels. . . . Thou, trader, shouldst trust God that He will find thee a livelihood with true winnings, for so much hath He promised thee with His divine mouth. Yet now thou swearest so loudly how good thy wares are, and what profit thou givest the buyer thereby; more than ten or thirty times takest thou the names of all the saints in vain—God and all His saints, for wares scarce worth five shillings!. . . And if thou wilt buy anything from simple folk, thou turnest all thy mind to see how thou mayest get it from him without money, and weavest many lies before his face; and thou biddest thy partner go to the fair also, and goest then a while away and sayest to thy partner what thou wilt give the man for his wares, and biddest him come and offer less. Then the simple country-fellow is affrighted and will gladly see thee come back; so thou gettest it untruly from him, and swearest all the while: "Of a truth," thou sayest, "by all the saints, no man will give thee so much for these as I!" Yet another would have given more. If thou wouldst keep thyself free from mortal sin in trade, see that thou swear not. Thou shouldst say: "If thou wilt not buy it, perchance another will": and should thus sell honestly without lie or deceit. Thus should a man keep himself in trade; for many thousand souls are damned thereby, seeing that there is so much fraud and falsehood and blasphemy that no man can tell it.

Moreover, the regulations to secure uniformity of workmanship and materials were not favourable to invention; it is a striking fact that, though Marco Polo described the Chinese printed banknotes before 1300, at least 120 years passed before men began, in Europe, even so elementary an imitation as to print little figures of saints on paper. It is doubtful whether artificial silk, for instance, could ever have fought its way through the medieval gild regulations in the face of established silk-merchants whose interests were against it. The religious gilds were framed to procure certain spiritual advantages: masses and prayers for the living, and for members' souls in purgatory or for their relations. But almost all gilds were partly religious, attending occasional services in common, and sometimes paying the whole stipend of a chaplain. All, again, insisted on a certain standard of behaviour; you were fined for coming to a meeting without shoes or stockings, or for ill-behaviour; and, if two members quarrelled, the gild strove for reconciliation. Two of the Leicester Merchants' Gild fought publicly at Boston Fair; their fellow-members fined them a barrel of beer, to be drunk by the gild. The punishment is suggestive; in fact, if the aims of the gilds were not always far-sighted, or their discipline always effectual, that was partly due to the conditions of society in general at that time. For instance, we have the coldest documentary evidence for the fact that, whereas there were definite statutory fines for different breaches of the trading regulations, the magistrates did not even attempt to enforce anything like the full penalties, and, of what they inflicted in word, not one-quarter was actually extracted from the offenders. Here, for instance, is Mr W. Hudson's analysis of the records of the leet-court at Norwich in 1289. The fines, themselves far more lenient than the law prescribed, varied from 3*d.* to 4*s.* The total for the year was £72. 18*s.* 10*d.*: that was the sum decreed by the court. But the collectors, even when this sum was several months overdue, could only account for £17. 0*s.* 2*d.*

It is clear [writes Mr Hudson] that, however efficient the system was in preventing offences from passing undetected, it did not do much to deter offenders from repeating them. Again, by far the most fertile source of municipal profit was the amercement of those who had been guilty of breaches of the assize of ale. The assize of bread is little mentioned. Perhaps it was dealt with in some other way. The price of ale was fixed according to the price of wheat. Almost every housewife of the leading families brewed ale and sold it to her neighbours, and invariably charged more than the fixed price. The authorities evidently expected this course to be taken, for these ladies were regularly presented and amerced every year for the same offence, paid their amercements and went away to go through the same process in the future as in the past. Much the same course was pursued by other trades and occupations. Fishmongers, tanners, poulterers, cooks, etc., are fined wholesale year after year for breaking every by-law that concerned their business. In short, instead of a trader (as now) taking out a license to do his business on certain conditions which he is expected to keep, he was bound by conditions which he was expected to break and afterwards fined for the breach. The same financial result was attained or aimed at by a different method.[1]

[1] *Records of the City of Norwich*, I, cxxxviii.

The first Crusade occurred at the very beginning of our period, and the Crusades gave a great impulse to trade. The restless energy of the Normans, who had settled down from piracy to comparative civilisation, accounts for a good deal. They threw themselves into the adventure of religious pilgrimage as they had thrown themselves hitherto into warfare; and pilgrimage and warfare, in those days, went very naturally hand in hand. Pilgrims were not always very patient folk, nor, again, were the lowlands always very orderly, let alone the mountain passes; it was common, therefore, to go in large armed caravans; and, as Gibbon puts it, robbers who were attracted by the garb of the pilgrim might find themselves punished by the arm of a warrior. But England, in spite of her seafaring traditions inherited from the Saxons and the Danes and the Normans, did not on the whole lead the way in the widest adventures by sea. Chaucer describes the skipper who rode in his company on the pilgrimage to Canterbury as a man of long experience; "by many a tempest had his beard been shaken"; yet apparently the farthest limits of his voyages had been Jutland in the north-east, and Cape Finisterre in Spain. The ships were small, and generally undecked or half-decked; the mariner's compass did not find its way to Europe till about A.D. 1150; and even then its use grew very slowly, so that sailors seldom ventured far out of sight of land. Many of them knew that the earth was round, but it was often believed that all the southern hemisphere was sea, except for one mountain in the very centre, on which was the Earthly Paradise, exactly opposite to Jerusalem in our hemisphere. To realise how far earth and sea were still unknown, and what terrible things were naturally believed about these mysterious regions, you must dip into Sir John Maundeville's *Travels*. Volcanoes are the different mouths of hell. The ruins of Babylon and the Pyramids swarm with dragons, serpents, and venomous beasts. In some parts there are giants forty cubits high; but Sir John has not seen these with his own eyes: "for I had no lust to go to those parts, because no man cometh to that isle but he will be devoured anon". One of his most frequent remarks, when he comes to describe some fresh tribe, is "they are of a right felonious and accursed nature", and "they eat man's flesh". He is a great literary artist, and exploits this pleasant shudder of danger to the full. Sometimes a hint is enough, as in the itinerary to the Holy Land: "And we go through the land of this lord, through a city that is called Cypron, and by the castle of Nease-borough, and by the Evil Town, which is situated towards the end of Hungary". Even much later, in Elizabeth's reign, the captain of a great ship which had to cross the Baltic from Riga to Lübeck warned his passengers of the danger, not only from pirates, but also from "monsters of the deep".[1] Yet a few Englishmen are on record as adventurous navigators in distant seas; and the nation, as a whole, showed great activity within its own narrower limits. The Channel itself was

[1] For the whole extract see my *Life in the Middle Ages*, III, 9.

often a great field for adventure, with those small boats and in the state of international feeling which reigned in those days. We read of a fighting noble whose boat took fifteen days to cross the Channel, and he himself so sick that he was never the same man again.[1] King John of France was once tossing eleven days between Bordeaux and Sandwich; and Edward III had one Channel passage so abominable that he could only ascribe it to successful witchcraft on the part of the French. Moreover, every sailor in the Channel was accustomed to play a privateer's part in war-time, and, too often, a pirate's part when he had not the excuse of open war. Chaucer puts it frankly in describing his Shipman;

> If that he fought, and had the higher hand,
> By water he sent them home by every land.

i.e. he threw the rival crew overboard. In this Channel adventure and Channel warfare England stood very well; on the whole, we generally commanded the narrow seas. But for wider adventure within our period, we must look to the Italian travellers and the Portuguese mariners.

The earliest record of these travels to the Far East come from Franciscan friars; of these, the best known are John of Piano Carpini, William of Rubruk, and Odoric of Perdenone. John, a man of noble birth, started in 1245 on his missionary journey; the year in which Westminster Abbey church, as we see it, was

----

[1] Macaulay's *Froissart*, p. 83; cf. pp. 134, 359.

begun. He was less a missionary in the strictest sense than a religious political agent; the Pope sent him to the Tartars in the hope that he might not only get them as allies instead of enemies in the great wars between Christians and Mohammedans, but might also persuade them to accept the religious supremacy of the Roman Church. For this sacred cause John and another Franciscan, his companion, braved, as he truly tells us, hunger and thirst, heat and cold, bodily exhaustion and ridicule, captivity and death; and, in fact, they not only braved but also suffered everything except prison and death. Medieval travel was not very easy under any conditions, and least of all for a missionary to the East. Almost at the be-

An aristocratic carriage in the early fourteenth century
(from the Louterell Psalter)

ginning, in Southern Russia, John became "feeble almost unto death"; but he pushed on, stronger in faith than in practical sagacity. The two friars rode hard, with a change of five horses a day; they were half-starved, since the Tartars feed so much upon flesh, and these missionaries were bound to avoid flesh in Lent and on fast-days. They fought their way through snowstorms in the highlands of Central Asia, and at last reached the court of the Tartar emperor on July 22, after a journey of nearly a year and a half. Here they were amazed at the multitude of ambassadors who came to congratulate the emperor, bringing with them "more than 500 carts which were all full of silver and gold and silk garments"; one single provincial governor offered a flock of camels all covered with the richest brocades. At the court, again, they were half-starved; on the homeward journey they often had to lie out in the snow all night; and, though they brought back letters from the emperor to the Pope, these contained nothing of political value.

At this we can hardly wonder, when we realise that John had not taken the precaution of learning anything of the Tartar language, either before or during the journey. William of Rubruk, another Franciscan, took the same journey in 1253, the year in which the great windows of Westminster Abbey chapter-house were finished. He went as an envoy from St Louis, King of France. His sufferings were similar to John's, with one extra inconvenience; for he confesses to being very corpulent, so that he suffered much on horseback.

To quote him textually, in Hakluyt's racy old translation,

Of twenty or thirty horses we had alwayes the woorst, because wee were strangers. For every one tooke their choice of the best horses before us. They provided mee alwaies of a strong horse, because I was very corpulent and heavy: but whether he ambled a gentle pase or no, I durst not make any question. Neither yet durst I complaine, although he trotted full sore. But every man must be contented with his lot as it fell. Whereupon wee were exceedingly troubled: for oftentimes our horses were tired before we could come at any people. And then wee were constrained to beate and whip on our horses, and to lay our garments upon other emptie horses: yea and some-times two of us to ride upon one horse. Of hunger and thirst, colde and wearinesse, there was no end. For they gave us no victuals, but onely in the evening. In the morning they used to give us a little drinke, or some sodden Millet to sup off. In the evening they bestowed flesh upon us, as namely, a shoulder and breast of rams mutton, and every man a measured quantitie of broath to drinke.... Sometimes we were faine to eate flesh half sodden, or almost rawe, and all for want of fewel to seethe it withal: especially when we lay in the fields, or were benighted before we came at our iourneis end: because we could not then conveniently gather together the doung of horses or oxen: for other fewel we found but seldome, except perhaps a few thornes in some places.

Two generations later, Odoric of Perdenone went still farther. Travelling by ship from port to port in the Eastern seas, he arrived at Canton; thence he went to Amoy, Fuchow, Hangchow, Nanking and Peking.

99

He gives startling but veracious descriptions of the wonders of China; he has little to tell us of missionary work in the strictest sense; but, on his return home, he was worshipped as a saint and credited with having baptized 20,000 heathens; for he probably served one of the fairly numerous churches in China which had been founded by John of Monte Corvino, another Franciscan, in about 1292.

John of Monte Corvino and his fellow-missionaries did, of course, learn the language. They had probably noticed how certain merchants had succeeded where the earlier missionaries had failed; and from those merchants they learned business methods. By far the best known of the merchants is the Venetian, Marco Polo. His father and uncle had started in 1260 to trade in China, and had come home. In 1271 they started again, taking with them Marco, a boy of about 16. The Pope sent two Dominican friars with them as missionaries; but these men turned back on hearing that there were wars in Armenia. The three merchants, however, were not to be daunted; they worked their way across Central Asia, faced the intense cold of the loftiest table-land in the world, and, after three-and-a-half years, reached the Khan's court. Marco got home to Venice, through a romantic chance, in 1295, after four-and-twenty years of travel and trading. His kinsfolk (we are told) refused to recognise him in the person of this weather-beaten and travel-stained stranger. So he ripped open his shabby cloak, and displayed such a profusion of jewels as convinced these Venetian business-folk at once. No doubt the Polos did work their way through travel and trade by keeping hidden stores of jewels about their person; but we may shudder to think what risks they ran of having their throats cut at any moment. Nobody can realise the foundations of medieval trade until he has grasped the fact that the merchant of those days was indeed a Merchant Adventurer. When men complain that we of the twentieth century live in a hustling, restless age, they say that the poor man will do anything nowadays in order to grow rich, and the rich man will do anything in order to grow richer. If that is true now, it was, if possible, even truer in the past. The Almighty Dollar has never had more power than it had, for instance, in Marco Polo's day; nor, again, was there ever more trickery in trade. For what Berthold of Regensburg tells us in the thirteenth century is fully borne out by Chaucer's contemporaries Gower and Bromyard, and, it may practically be said, by every moralist of the Middle Ages. I have quoted Gower's evidence briefly on p. 125 of *Chaucer and his England*.

CHAPTER VIII

Scholasticism and Free-Thought

AFTER these glimpses of social and economic life in the Middle Ages, let us go back for a while to trace the development of thought. We have seen how much of ancient thought was naturally cast overboard by the early Christians and in the Dark Ages; let us note now how things went in the Middle Ages proper, when the barbarian invaders had settled down, and the Church was gradually civilising them, yet not without certain compromises which affected the whole course of medieval civilisation, if indeed they may not still be traced in modern society.

It was long believed, partly on the authority of Michelet (a great and most suggestive French historian who on this point was misled by one exaggerated sentence of the chronicler Ralph Glaber), that there had been a universal expectation of the world's end in or about A.D. 1000. There was in fact a somewhat heightened expectation then, but not much more definite than those to which St Augustine bears testimony in his own lifetime; therefore, as the years passed after 1000, nothing remained but the general expectation of the Second Advent, exercising a real influence on men's thoughts, often subordinating their views of this world to their views of the next, reasonably operative in the minds of true and consistent thinkers, vaguely operative in the popular mind, and steadily but slowly weakening as time went on. After that crucial year, there were no more important barbarian invasions; Europe was fast settling down, reconstruction was possible; and, when once the process had begun, it proceeded steadily. This forward movement of the year 1000, therefore, which was running with full force about the middle of the next century, was a very real revival, comparable to that later revival which we call the Renaissance. Men attacked with confidence the great and fundamental problems of Predestination and Free Will, of the Origin of Evil, of the Atonement, of Christ's Real Presence in the Eucharist. Abailard now, like Johannes Scotus Eriugena in the ninth century, showed considerable independence of the patristic tradition; he even broke away altogether from legalistic traditions as to Redemption through Christ: the Saviour's blood (he argued) was not a "price" paid to Satan for man's soul, which had been forfeited through Adam's sin, but a sacrifice through which "God bound Himself (to us) more fully than before by love"; we have here an anticipation of Dante's splendid description of love that compels love in return—"love that sets no lover free from loving".

To St Bernard, Abailard's presumption in applying reason to theology was intolerable; this man "is content to see nothing through a glass darkly, but must behold all face to face". Bernard secured Abailard's official condemnation; but the clock could not be set back, and Abailard's method finally triumphed in an age of superabundant energy and of thirst for knowledge. All inquiry was welcomed, so long as it kept within the limits clearly marked by the Bible and by the great councils. We have seen how the medieval Church held the plenary inspiration of the Bible as firmly, perhaps, as any great religious denomination has ever held it.

The decrees of the general councils were treated with scarcely less respect; again, few thinkers dared flatly to contradict any of the great Fathers, among whom St Ambrose, St Augustine, St Jerome and St Gregory were placed in a class above the rest. But, within those limits, argument and discussion were strongly encouraged by what we may call this medieval Renaissance. Abailard's dialectical method was followed by his pupil Peter Lombard, bishop of Paris, who is generally counted as the first of the schoolmen. The method had been first developed in Abailard's *Sic et Non* ("Yes and No"). In that remarkable book, prefaced by a still more remarkable introduction on the interpretation of Scripture, Abailard marshals, for comparison's sake, texts from the Bible or the Fathers which seem to contradict each other, and thus to afford fertile subjects for discussion: hence the title of the work. Peter Lombard elaborated this in his *Sentences*, a fuller collection in which he attempts what Abailard had avoided, viz. the formal reconciliation of these apparently conflicting texts. This book of the

104

1219-1294

Sentences soon became the classical text-book for theologians; Roger Bacon complains that, already in his
own day, it had almost superseded the study of the
Bible as a whole; that men argued from these texts
wrenched from their context, instead of familiarising
themselves with the complete body of Scriptures.

This brings us to Scholasticism. The clearest definition of this word is indicated by its etymology and its
history. It was the philosophy and the theology of
the Schools, among which, in medieval parlance, the
Universities stood first. In these new thinking-shops,
which grew up at the end of the twelfth century, work
was carried on after the methods natural to a comparatively bookless but book-hungry age. The teacher
alone, normally, had his text-book; this he discussed
with his class after the fashion of Socrates, that is,
mainly by catechetical and dialectical methods. To the
end, medieval teaching retained traces of its original
dialectical form, seen at its best in such a book as the
1225-1
Summa Theologiae of St Thomas Aquinas. There, each
article is divided into four parts. First, the author
rehearses all the arguments worth considering against
what he himself judges to be the true conclusion. Then
he rehearses those which make for it. He then delivers
his own formal judgment. Lastly, he undertakes to
explain away, one by one, the apparent objections
contained in his first list of arguments. In other words,
he plays four different parts—plaintiff, defendant,
judge, and judge of appeal. And this characteristic
method worked upon a characteristic body of subject-

matter—the Bible, the Fathers and Aristotle, with certain infiltrations of Plato, mainly through the neo-Platonists. A good deal of Aristotle had survived even through the Dark Ages, in the translations of Boethius. At the end of the twelfth century the complete Aristotle came in, first through translations from Arabic versions and commentaries, and later through direct versions from the Greek, at the instigation of scholars like Aquinas.

We may take, as a fair example of the scholastic method, St Thomas's discussion of the treatment of heretics. It must be remembered that on certain points the orthodox theologian of that day had no choice; he was not permitted to doubt for one moment anything which seemed to have received the sanction of Church authority. Therefore St Thomas based himself necessarily on the medieval notions of heaven and hell, and on the assumption that, at a man's last breath, the one question which did most in Western Europe to decide between an eternity of indescribable bliss or unspeakable torment was the question whether he died in the Roman Catholic faith. He argues, therefore, as follows (2ª 2ᵃᵉ Q. X and XI). Unbelief is the worst of sins. Though the unbelief of pagans or Jews diverges farther from the truth than that of heretics, yet the heretic is more sinful than they are. And this is important for the question of religious compulsion; for, whereas those who never were Christians may not be coerced into Christianity, yet heretics and apostates must be compelled, even by bodily force, to fulfil what they have implicitly promised. The faithful may have business dealings with pagans and Jews, but not with heretics. No class of unbelievers, however, may be suffered to command orthodox Christians; thus a Jew may not have a Christian servant. The religious rites of unbelievers may be tolerated in so far as they support true Christian worship—*e.g.* those Jewish rites which prefigure the Christian dispensation—but no others. The young children of unbelievers must not be baptised against their parents' will. Though heretics do not deserve any toleration whatever, yet they should be warned once and twice: if, after that, they still pertinaciously cling to their heresy, then it is our duty to cut them off from the world by death: for, if we kill false coiners and other felons, still more are we bound to kill pertinacious heretics. A heretic, however often he may have relapsed, must never be denied *spiritual* forgiveness on his repentance and return to the Church, but *temporal* forgiveness can be extended to him only once: if, after that, he relapses, he has so earned death and forfeit of his goods that no penitence can now save him; the good of the whole community must outweigh all considerations of mercy to this individual.

All this, it will be seen, is deduced by rigorous logic from the fundamental assumptions of medieval orthodoxy. We cannot escape from Aquinas's conclusions except by denying or tacitly ignoring his premises: the conclusions are implicit in those premises.

This combination of method and subject-matter, once clearly grasped, not only defines the word

Scholasticism, but explains the main characteristics of medieval philosophy. The medieval agrees with the ancient philosophy in its reliance upon the dialectical method, but differs from it as basing itself formally upon a certain body of traditional thought, most of which it was very dangerous, if not absolutely forbidden, to contradict. This restriction was less narrow than it might seem to us; there was far more liberty in the medieval schools than there has been in the papal schools since the Council of Trent, as Cardinal Newman has insisted with even exaggerated emphasis. Yet it was a very real restriction, and it differentiates Scholasticism even more sharply from modern than from ancient philosophy. Even the most original and most audacious of the medieval Scholastics were compelled to defer to tradition to an extent which would have been repudiated by Aristotle and Plato almost as emphatically as by the non-theological philosophers of modern times. William of Ockham, the greatest of the later Scholastics, was not only bold and original, but an actual and declared rebel against the Papacy of his day (1300–1350); yet in his assertions of freedom he is hesitating in comparison with his contemporary, the physician Marsilius of Padua. Still, within the permitted limits, thought was extremely active for many generations. An early provincial minister was shocked to hear his Franciscan friars at Oxford disputing on the question "Whether God exists". St Thomas, within the first ten "quaestiones" of his *Summa Theologiae*, feels called upon to discuss whether God exists, whether He be perfect, whether He be the Highest Good, whether He be Infinite, whether He be Eternal, and to solve all objections before passing on.

There were many, however, who could not feel themselves to have solved these objections. Medieval Christendom, in spite of reactionary protests, was too vigorous not to direct the full force of human reason to discussion within the permitted limits, and here Abailard was entirely justified against St Bernard and the mystical school of St Victor. But this exercise of reason was bound to cause many conflicts between the enquiring mind and the official limitations; and there St Bernard was perfectly right. Whether Abailard foresaw this result or not (and, if we may believe his own words, he anticipated no real danger to the Faith), this revival of learning and of speculation did breed a great deal of heterodoxy. Aristotle himself is difficult enough to reconcile, in many places, with Christianity; still less reconcilable were his Arabic translators and commentators, of whom Averroës was the most popular at Paris. Therefore the Council of Sens in 1210 prohibited university study of Aristotle's works on natural science; the papal legate repeated this prohibition in 1215; in 1231 the Pope renewed it "until they should have been examined and purged". For this purpose he nominated a commission, but, as Father Mandonnet points out, the very attempt betrayed imperfect knowledge of Aristotle. The decree was renewed in 1263; but the official expurgation never took place, as indeed it could not, since Aristotle's treatises are too closely reasoned and too clearly expressed to be capable of paste-and-scissors treatment. All this while, "as a matter of fact, in spite of the law, Aristotle had more or less rapidly invaded the Schools of Paris and entered into the [regular] course of instruction".[1] In 1255 the University was prescribing virtually all of Aristotle, in so far as he was available, for its degree course.

It is not surprising, therefore, that these years betray a strong undercurrent of free thought in the modern sense. Amaury de Bène was condemned, and possibly burned, for pantheistic doctrines in about 1207; David de Dinant's writings were burned in 1210; and at the same time a batch of students were condemned to the stake or to perpetual imprisonment. Two or three of the most distinguished Parisian teachers were condemned in 1277, probably to lifelong imprisonment; one of them was Siger de Brabant, whom Dante places side by side with Thomas Aquinas in heaven, yet who undoubtedly taught Averroistic doctrines. By this time the Inquisition was in full blast, and the authorities rejected Siger's plea that a proposition might be true in philosophy, though false in theology. That plea still remained the last refuge of the free-thinker; a very interesting instance may be quoted from Oxford in 1382. A University teacher "strove to prove the opinion of Wycliff concerning the Sacrament of the Altar, and at length, when the Masters were congregated, he said in the presence of all that there is no

[1] H. Rashdall, *Universities of Europe*, 1st edition, I, pp. 68 ff.

idolatry like that of the Sacrament of the Altar—*quod non est idolatria nisi in Sacramento Altaris*. Yet the Chancellor said nothing to him but 'Now thou speakest as a philosopher'". In other words, theologically this is a heresy, but we will pass it as philosophical discussion.[1] But though this, and the periodic condemnation of heterodox thinkers at different universities, enables us to guess what still went on under the surface, yet no medieval thinker could openly transgress the main conventional limits, unless here and there some fortunate accident might protect him.

The Blessed Joachim of Fiore did indeed excogitate unchecked a theory of religious development which, in its full implications, would have done much to supersede the hierarchy and the sacraments; but, so soon as his disciples multiplied and a Parisian teacher openly drew the logical inferences, this provoked papal condemnation.[2] Another Professor at Paris, Nicholas de Ultricuria, anticipated the philosophic doubts of Berkeley and Hume; thirty-two of his propositions were briefly rehearsed and formally condemned at the papal court in 1346; he duly retracted, and was rewarded within two years with the Deanery of Metz; it is only this condemnation which has by chance preserved a record of his teaching. There we have only a specially clear example of that which meets us everywhere in vaguer indications. Free thought was driven underground; it could not form a school wherever

[1] *Fasciculi Zizaniorum*, R.S., p. 307.
[2] I have given the story briefly in *Five Centuries of Religion*, II, c. vii.

the Inquisition was strong; yet it could not be altogether exorcised. As time went on, and as culture and the citizen class spread, it even stalked abroad again. Florence, one of the most civilised cities, was also one of the least orthodox; Dante fills a whole circle of his Inferno with men who had died in disbelief of the soul's immortality. In the next generation, Petrarch complained that "modern philosophers", in Venice, scoffed at the orthodox as old-fashioned fools. "But that they fear punishment from men more than God's vengeance, they would dare to attack not only Plato's doctrine of creation, but Moses and his Genesis, and the Catholic faith and the holy doctrine of Christ. When this fear no longer restrains them, in their secret meetings, they mock at Christ and worship Aristotle, whom they do not understand."[1] Sacchetti, Chaucer's contemporary, has much to say about infidelity in the Florence of his day; his whole sermon, no. XLIII, is devoted to this subject. The University of Padua became a focus of Averroism; and thence it spread over all northern Italy. By the beginning of the sixteenth century the question of immortality was discussed even at the papal court; but then the Pope was Leo X, and the Renaissance had loosed a flood of scepticism.

Heresy was still contraband, but this prohibition law, like others of the kind, was being more and more openly violated. No organised rebellion was yet possible; the weaker offenders were sometimes caught

[1] Quoted in E. Renan, *Averroës*, p. 335.

and punished; sometimes even the stronger; but there was increasing defiance among the more powerful, so long as they had tact enough not to challenge prosecution too clearly, and wealth or rank enough to make them dangerous. Moreover, this resultant free thought, like other contraband articles, was often not of the purest quality. The admitted decay of philosophy in the later Middle Ages—in spite of great names here and there, such as Nicholas of Cues and Gabriel Biel—was in a great measure due to the want of real freedom. Wycliffite prosecutions killed the earlier originality of Oxford University; it became almost impossible for any teacher to strike a just mean between irresponsible negation and docile adherence to the old well-worn ruts. Such, then, were the obstacles to progress in philosophy and theology.

CHAPTER IX

Law and Politics

LAW was an important subject at nearly all the universities; Bologna was as celebrated for its legists as Paris for its divines. But even more influential, perhaps, and certainly more distinctively medieval, was the Canon Law. From the time when Constantine made Christianity the State religion, emperors were naturally called upon to legislate fairly frequently in protection or in regulation of the ecclesiastical corporation. In 438 the Theodosian code practically decreed outlawry against all heretics. At about the same time Valentinian III granted the pope legislative power over the Church in his own, the Western, half of the Empire. Many collections were made, more or less fortuitously, embodying imperial, conciliar and papal decrees concerning the Church; the best of these was made by a Roman monk, Dionysius Exiguus, about the year 500, from which collection even popes began to quote. Into this volume were thrust the Forged Donation of Constantine and the False Decretals.

The former forgery was fully developed about A.D. 750; it purported to be a decree of Constantine, who recited a fable of having been cured of leprosy by Pope Sylvester I, in gratitude for which he now bestows on the popes the sovereignty over Italy and the

West. Gregory the Great, in whose time the fable had first grown up, had contemptuously ignored it; but five generations later it was possible for even the best educated clergy to accept in complete innocence this "most stupendous of all medieval forgeries". A century after the Forged Donation came the Forged Decretals (890). This collection, edited under the name of Isidorus Mercator, was an astounding mass of falsely ascribed or forged documents, leavened with a sprinkling of genuine which lent a sort of respectability to the rest. Yet, though nobody knew anything of this reputed Isidorus Mercator, and here and there, in the first few months, a prelate might refuse to recognise them, they soon acquired an authority almost as undisputed as Holy Writ. Nicholas I silenced all doubts in a decretal which was later embodied in Canon Law; thenceforward this forgery, like the Donation, was unquestioned until about 1450, when the humanist Laurentius Valla and the philosopher Nicholas of Cues ventured to express very plain doubts. It is true that these forgeries answered very closely to the ideas which had grown up during the previous few centuries; step by step, the popes had openly claimed or quietly taken for granted, one by one, as the generations went on, most or all of the points which the Forged Decretals state so plainly. But the step from gradual encroachment in practice to formal documentary acknowledgment is a wide and most important step. The papal claims, like the British occupation of India and of Egypt or the American occupation of Cuba, had been frequently opposed; and the Forged Decretals did as much for the popes as would be done for Britain if we could make the world believe that our occupation of Egypt had reposed on a definite gift from the Caliph, and that a series of orthodox Mahometan laws had granted us free action everywhere and for all time in that country. And, in any case, the fact that they could be so boldly invented in the chancery of a Frankish bishop, so suddenly thrust upon the world, so definitely accepted by a very able pope, and obeyed without question for seven centuries, is one of the most characteristic points in the history of the medieval mind.

With the revival of Roman law at Bologna, early in the twelfth century, came a corresponding stimulus to Church law. A monk called Gratian, probably in the year 1142, undertook to bring some sort of order into this subject; for, meanwhile, all kinds of genuine decrees had been thrust in since these two great forgeries, and other more or less authoritative collections had been attempted. The very title of Gratian's work indicates his main object: *A Concordance of Discordant Canons*; but, for convenience, the book has always borne the briefer title of Gratian's *Decretum*. Here, at last, we find some attempt at scientific synthesis. The decrees are arranged according to their subject-matter after the model of civil law; again, Gratian added comments of his own with the object of reconciling the numerous inconsistencies and contradictions. This book, though not formally published by the popes, was from the first utilised by them in public, and never repudiated. When, in 1234, Gregory IX ordered a fresh and official collection of papal decretals, that volume was avowedly published as a continuation of Gratian. Similar collections were added during the next century; the last medieval pope who acted thus was John XXII in 1317.

By that time it was evident that such collections were clashing more and more with national state laws and with growing national self-consciousness. A semi-official appendix, however, was added in 1490, under the title of *Extravagantes*. This, then, completed the *Corpus Juris Canonici* (Body of Canon Law), which thus consisted of Gratian, the officially added decretals, and the *Extravagantes*. A commission of cardinals and professors, sitting under three popes, produced a standard text of this *Corpus*, which was published by order of Gregory XIII in 1582. Here again, therefore, were certain definite limits within which medieval thought was restricted by law, and often confined in fact.

The natural result was that hard thinking often degenerated into verbal quibbles; research and thought were subordinated to forensic display. "Medieval education", says Rashdall, "was at once too dogmatic and too disputatious". But it did much to fashion tools for thought and speech; many of our commonest and most indispensable abstract words, such as "quality" and "quantity", were partly or wholly invented by the Scholastics. Therefore, while the great thinkers of the earlier period still command respectful attention from metaphysicians and theologians, "the rapid multiplication of universities during the fourteenth and fifteenth centuries was largely due to a direct demand for highly-educated lawyers and administrators". Men there learned habits of steady and intense application; they were there equipped to deal skilfully, for their own purposes, with such facts as it suited them or their fellows to recognise; but there was far too little of that impartial observation of concrete facts, without which the most brilliant abstractions are likely to mislead us. The public study of medicine was forbidden to monks and friars; it is a great mistake to imagine that the cloistered clergy were the physicians of the Middle Ages. When we find a physician among the cloistered clergy—and such cases are rare, considering the enormous mass of records which has survived—there is nearly always some indication that the man had been a physician in "the world", before he took the vows. St Francis and his earliest companions did indeed sometimes tend lepers; but there is no evidence whatever for friars as regular attendants in leper-hospitals. At the other hospitals, which were alms-houses also, the directors were generally, in the later medieval centuries, Canons Regular of St Augustine, and the nurses, women vowed to celibacy; but there was much variety from house to house. Even when the Warden or Brethren were cloistered clergy, they seldom tended the sick themselves; such physical contact was left to the sisters or the lay-brethren. These institutions were generally as much alms-houses as hospitals in the modern sense. St John's at Oxford may be taken as fairly typical; the staff consisted there of three chaplains, Augustinians, of whom one was Master, with six lay-brethren and six sisters.[1] But in Italy, from very early times at least, the hospitals were very often under civic management, as they had been under the ancient empire. In other countries also, the care of rich and poor was more and more definitely taken in hand by the lay authorities during the last few generations before the Reformation. At Strassburg, about 1500, the citizens even forbade the reception of clergy as patients into the city hospitals, or the services of nuns as attendants. In England, the founder of a school at Sevenoaks prescribed that the master should not be in holy orders (A.D. 1432). In 1443, a London citizen founded a school to be governed by the Mercers' Company; and when Colet, Dean of St Paul's, refounded his Cathedral school, he not only followed this example but gave plain reasons for it.

In one other important field the general public were deeply interested. Written records being comparatively rare, a great deal of legal testimony depended upon visual and oral testimony. Great pains, therefore, were sometimes taken to ensure the desired notoriety. No parochial marriage registers, for instance, existed; and therefore the bulk of the marriage ceremony took place not inside the church, but outside, at the door, in order that it might be seen by the greatest possible

[1] R. M. Clay, *The Medieval Hospitals of England*, pp. 149-156.

number of witnesses. Thus Chaucer's Wife of Bath records complacently the number of husbands whom she had had "at the church door". On other occasions the witnesses were chosen as young as possible, in order that their testimony might last as late as possible. One device was to buy a large quantity of cherries and scatter them among the children, explaining solemnly first what was this occasion which brought them so pleasant a windfall. Equally popular from the legal point of view, if not from that of the witnesses, was an entirely contrary procedure; one or more children were so solemnly and so thoroughly whipped on the occasion that it might be taken for granted they would never forget. A great Norman noble consecrated a munificent gift of land to a monastery by casting his young son, clad in a rich fur cloak, into the water.

But, to return to medicine, much of it was naturally of a very simple character. One or more monks in a monastery probably knew enough to assist their fellows in the infirmary with herbs and poultices and common-sense rules of diet; it is not unusual to find notes of this kind, with recipes, scribbled on the fly-leaves of books. Nuns, again, though they were nominally very strictly enclosed, are sometimes to be found ministering thus, by which they doubtless earned gifts from the rich and thanks from the poor. The wise woman of the village, again, had her recipes and her charms; and the ordinary housewife had traditional recipes. But, for scientific medicine, the Middle Ages were mainly dependent upon the Greeks of antiquity, either in

Marriage at the church door

direct translations or in infiltrations through Jewish or
Arabic writers. The Church frowned upon anatomy,
and it was little practised; among modern students,
even those who are most in sympathy with medieval
thought, it is generally confessed that the Universities
of that age spent too much time and energy on meta-
physics, and too little on the direct observation of
natural phenomena, or on the exact record of facts of
any kind. It is true that the chroniclers have left us
many valuable records, yet there were no schools of
geography or history; moreover there was a fatal
neglect of languages, mathematics and the physical
sciences. St Thomas Aquinas, in his demonstration of
the truth of Christianity against the heathen, appeals to
two facts, which he says are equally familiar to the
learned, yet equally inexplicable to the vulgar herd:
"It seemeth marvellous to ignorant folk that the
magnet draweth iron, or that a little fish holdeth back
a ship"—this "little fish" was the fabulous remora,
only a foot long, yet able by suction to hold the greatest
vessels![1] The most remarkable artists' manual of the
later Middle Ages, by Cennino Cennini of Florence,
which undertakes to teach us the true proportions of
the human figure, and to mould the whole body of a
man or woman from the life, assures us that "a man
has on his left side one rib less than a woman".

This habitual carelessness was a terrible encourage-
ment to forgery: "Such great persons, such powerful

[1] *Summa contra Gentiles*, lib. III, c. 102. Cf. my *Social Life in Britain*,
p. 531.

societies, were accomplices in falsification that it required a rare share of public spirit for a humble critic to expose too coarsely their methods of manipulating documents", writes Professor Tout in *Medieval Forgers and Forgeries*.

Monastic chartularies contain large numbers of documents now admitted to be more or less definitely unauthentic; great medieval lawsuits were frequently prosecuted through forgeries. In 1432 the University of Cambridge successfully asserted its independence against the Bishop of Ely at the great Barnwell Trial by means of a forged charter of Pope Honorius I, who was made to assert that, having himself studied at Cambridge, he had been moved by gratitude to grant this privilege of exemption in 624, nearly six centuries before the University was actually founded! F. W. Maitland, referring to the fictions by which Oxford and Cambridge each tried to prove its superior antiquity, wrote: "The earliest of all inter-University contests was a lying match". Indeed, no historical ignorance was impossible even in the highest quarters. Pope Gregory II, in his letter to the iconoclastic emperor, asserts in all innocence that the Apostles had been image-worshippers.[1]

Here, medieval ignorance was very largely due to the scarcity of books and their imperfect diffusion; "for various reasons (as Professor C. H. Haskins has pointed out) books had very little independent movement of their own". The chronicle which was partly

[1] Migne, *Pat. Lat.*, vol. LXXXIX, col. 514 C.

copied and partly written by Matthew Paris is of supreme value, yet very few copies ever existed outside its native monastery of St Albans. The idea that monks were constantly transcribing will not bear the test of facts; the market was mainly supplied by hired scribes; and, though there may have been a few exceptions, the Middle Ages never really adopted that system which we know to have been used in classical antiquity, of multiplying books by dictating to a class. Hence, though the scribe was paid only an artisan's wages, books were always dear: a Bible often cost more than a priest's whole yearly income, and the ordinary parish priest who possessed a copy was very rare indeed. Chaucer's Clerk of Oxenforde, for all that he had spent of his own and from his friends, had only twenty books; Bernard of Chartres, the most distinguished teacher in the classical revival of the twelfth century, left all his library to the Cathedral; it comprised twenty-four volumes.

Again, the use of Latin as a universal language had, with some real advantages, other very great drawbacks. It is an exaggeration to speak of Latin as ever becoming a real second vernacular, except perhaps in Italy and Spain. Even learned men, as we may tell from chance indications, thought their most intimate thoughts in the mother tongue. Though all University lectures were in Latin, and schools and colleges often paid a "lupus" (*i.e.* *wolf*; the nickname given to a scholar holding his scholarship by the tenure of acting as reporter against all fellow-scholars who lapsed into the vernacular), yet Universities were obliged to license grammar schools for the undergraduates who had too little Latin to follow the regular teaching. Only a small proportion of the priesthood were University graduates; orthodox contemporaries tell such stories of ignorance of Latin even among priests as would be scarcely credible if they were not borne out by occasional official records of examinations. A visitation of 1222, among seventeen dean and chapter livings of Sarum, shows us five priests who were unable to construe even the opening words of the first prayer in the Canon of the Mass, which is the essential portion of the Eucharistic service. Erasmus tells us of one of the best bishops of that day who attempted to remedy clerical ignorance, but finally gave up the hopeless attempt. We must therefore bear in mind that, all through the Middle Ages, there was a great mass of lower parish clergy who, in fact, knew little more than their parishioners. I have printed several of these clerical examination reports in *Life in the Middle Ages*, vol. II, pp. 39–48. They are as amusing as they are instructive.

Even in the highest University circles, it may be doubted whether a dozen people anywhere could sit round the fire and discuss the problems of life and death in Latin, with anything like the freedom and penetration of a similar group speaking to-day in their own language. Very few can have been the speakers who could bring out, or the hearers who could seize without excessive efforts, those finest shades of expression which test a man's exactness of thought and command of his native tongue. It must have been nearly always true that the man's deepest concepts were in his own language, while he expressed them in the formal language of the schools; and this is one reason why there were no clearly-separated national schools of philosophy in the Middle Ages. What thought gained in extension it lost in depth and in originality; the philosopher's ideas were not constantly cross-fertilised by the experiences and thoughts of common life. "The mother-tongue", said Herr Stresemann in his first speech before the League of Nations, "is the sanctuary of the soul". Many men have lost full command of their own native language without corresponding gain from any other; and it is no mere surmise, but a matter which can be proved by plain evidence, that this happened more often in the Middle Ages than to-day. Latin had its great use as a universal language; but, on the other hand, it helped to encourage conventionality; the ideas to which it gave easiest expression and widest circulation were too often stereotyped. Johann Busch, a distinguished German churchman of the fifteenth century, gives us in the midst of his Latin works a prayer which he had composed for his own private use at Mass, or instead of Mass when his attendance had been hindered. This prayer is in his native German; that was the language which, in his private thoughts, brought him nearest to God. So, again, with the great mystic Heinrich Suso (d. 1363). In his *Little Book of Eternal Wisdom*, he tells us that he writes his mystical thoughts in German, since it was in German that God had revealed them to him.

Political thought, as a separate social science, was unknown in the Middle Ages. It was a subsection of divinity or of law; and the political theorists were theologians or legists. Indeed, even the legist was compelled here to be something of a theologian, since the Bible was the one infallible authority, and the Fathers were often treated with almost equal respect. The book which became classical for all earlier medieval political theory, and kept much of its influence to the very end, was St Augustine's *City of God*. "City" and "State" were not yet definitely separate terms; men still thought and wrote to a great extent under the idea of the old city state; to St Augustine, the Roman Empire is a "civitas", so also is the Church, which claims a still more universal and less localised dominion. The book was called forth by Alaric's sack of Rome in A.D. 410. Under the shock of this catastrophe, St Jerome wrote to his friend Ageruchia: "If Rome falls, what is there that remains standing?" This, no doubt, would not have been Jerome's last word in any case; and with Augustine it was not even a passing mood. If the earthly state, founded on physical force, breaks down under pressure of superior force, yet the Heavenly State is still inviolate; men may destroy the body, but not the spirit. That contrast is the text of the whole book of *The City of God*. Reactionaries had frequently attributed all the sufferings of the later

Roman Empire to this new-fangled religion which she had adopted; and the fall of Rome revived a prophecy that Christianity would run only as many years as we count days; that the 365th year from its beginning would mark its final end. Therefore all the first half of the *City of God* is devoted to destructive criticism. Augustine shows how little the old gods had done to save Republican or Imperial Rome from bloodshed without and within, or from moral corruption; nay, how definitely these immoral deities, and the superstitions clinging to their cult, had fostered moral corruption, and therefore brought down the vengeance of God. Thence he passes to argue that the earthly state partakes necessarily of the corruption of fallen man; in Eden there would have been neither statecraft nor ownership; politics and property are the direct consequence of Adam's fall. Cain, the first murderer, is recorded also in the Bible to have founded the first city. The first great empire, Assyria, was founded by Nimrod, in whom the Middle Ages saw a gigantic antagonist of God. Rome itself was founded in a brother's blood; and she had since dyed her hands in the blood of the Saints. Rome's long reign had been part of God's plan; her victories over Carthage and other rivals had in a sense been God's victories, since He had chosen this worldly empire as a material foundation for His everlasting empire. Rome had been the "paidagogos"—half nurse, half tutor—to bring the growing world to Christ; that mission is now fulfilled, and even this sack of Rome in 410 is only one more bubble on the stream of time. The earthly city perishes as the body must perish; the City of God endures with the soul; and Augustine concludes with that text of triumphant consolation from the Epistle to the Hebrews: "There remaineth therefore a rest for the people of God".

The book deserves its reputation and its almost unparalleled influence. Its weakest point is that of its own and many succeeding ages: a fanciful, and even (the less sympathetic readers may feel) sometimes a reckless liberty of Biblical interpretation; such, for instance, as we have seen with Cain and Nimrod. But it is full of real learning; many important facts of Roman social history are known to us only through Augustine's quotations from older authors. And, above all, it is one of the earliest efforts, if not the very earliest, to construct a philosophy of history; to indicate one guiding thread through the vicissitudes of human events. Even those who are least inclined to accept Augustine's interpretations at their face value may yet acknowledge that, essentially, he was right; that the real interest of history is this eternal conflict of the ideal and the actual—of the state in which we live, and to which on the whole we loyally submit, and of that state which never has been realised, which perhaps never shall be, yet which, in a supreme crisis, may call upon us for an obedience even above the obedience we owe to human law. St Augustine tinged this with a dualism which is often implied in early Christian thought; an implication that the powers of good and evil are, in this world, very evenly balanced. He had begun as a Manichaean, and Manichaeanism is strongly dualistic; therefore his own personal experience tempted him even to exaggerate the dualistic element in Christianity; any reader may understand this by turning to his *Confessions*, the first real autobiography in all literature. But the ordinary facts of life force a certain amount of dualism upon all of us; common sense will freely echo Augustine's remark that two bad men must necessarily disagree and contend; that a good and a bad man must needs contend; that contention, therefore, can be eliminated only in a society in which all alike are good. Thus, life is a struggle between body and spirit, between darkness and light; this fact remains even when we have repudiated all the saint's exaggerations, and have done all that truth can do to soften the contrasts in this universe.

The political implications of *The City of God*, after the breakdown of central imperial authority, will be obvious. The Church, by this time, had strong and legitimate political claims; her organism, however definitely modelled on that of the State, was more elastic, in virtue of its greater spirituality. The breakdown of the civil authority had thrown upon her all responsibilities of social beneficence; even, in some cases, the upkeep of roads and bridges. These duties she shouldered, and reaped her natural reward; especially in proportion as the growing importance of the bishop of Rome focussed her elaborate organi-

sation upon him, almost as definitely as the still more
elaborate civil bureaucracy from which it was borrowed
had been focussed in the emperor's person. Therefore
in A.D. 800, when the Empire was revived in the West
under Charles the Great, it had already a serious
political rival in the Papacy; and upon this rivalry all
subsequent political thought of the Middle Ages is
more or less definitely hinged. The main lines of
discussion were naturally determined by *The City of
God*. It was assumed that Church and State were as
inseparable as soul and body, yet needing no less
careful and constant readjustment. Augustine, though
not always quite consistent, clearly recognises on the
whole the necessity of rendering unto Caesar the
things which are Caesar's; but there was much in this
book which lent itself easily to the support of papal
claims. Less than a century later (about A.D. 495)
Pope Gelasius made a memorable pronouncement.
In secular matters (he said) it is for the emperor to
make laws, and for the churchman to obey; but, in
matters of religious faith or ceremony, decision rests
with the pope. This Gelasian Concordat, as it has been
called, was observed by St Gregory the Great, the
converter of the Anglo-Saxons (590–604). He admitted that he was bound, as a subject, to promulgate
imperial laws, even while he protested against them
as trenching seriously upon Church privileges. His
words are so remarkable that they must be quoted in
full. Addressing the Emperor and his council, he
wrote: "I confess to my lords that I was sore afraid of

this law; for thereby the road to heaven is shut to many men....What am I but dust and a worm? Yet, feeling as I do that this law tends against God who made all, I cannot be silent before my lords....Being a man set under authority, I have caused this law aforesaid to be sent on to divers parts of the earth.... thus paying what I owed to both parties; for I have rendered obedience to the Emperor on the one side, while for God's sake I have spoken plainly that which I felt."

But, in the West, the clergy were almost the only guardians of written records; they alone, as a rule, could read and write; here again, therefore, if their real merits gave them a political advantage which they sometimes exploited to the utmost, this was a pardonable human failing. Nicholas I (858–867) violated the Gelasian Concordat, taking advantage of a passage in *The City of God*; it is for the sake of peace that men form themselves into a State; therefore, if the civil ruler, by misgovernment, fails to secure peace, it is the Church's duty to intervene, and to command where the Prince has broken down. A claim of this kind might obviously be construed to justify even the extremest papalistic doctrines. Therefore, as time went on, Gregory VII (1073–1085), exaggerating again from *The City of God*, claimed it as a self-evident truth that the State founded by Christ should dominate the State founded by Cain; the pope, therefore, may make and unmake princes. With Innocent III (1198–1216), a great canon lawyer, these principles were still further developed. Boniface VIII (1294–1303) made claims, we can scarcely say even greater, but expressed in more downright language, than any of his predecessors; all laws (he says) are enshrined in the casket of the papal breast; and again: "We declare most solemnly that subjection to the Roman Pontiff is an absolutely necessary condition of salvation for all human beings". This was in the famous bull *Unam Sanctam*, which, by nearly universal consent, is to be counted among the few clearly *ex cathedra*, and therefore infallible, utterances of the Papacy.[1] Boniface's exact words are: "Moreover, we declare that all human beings are subject to the Pontiff of Rome; and we assert, define and pronounce this tenet to be necessary to salvation". But here (a phenomenon common enough) the extremest verbal pretensions come when the reality is already beginning to decay. The Papacy, by this time, was pitted no longer against emperors who were more or less nominal rulers over a State comprising Germany, Austria, most of Italy and of the Low Countries, and parts of France, and among whose subjects, therefore, it was easy to sow division. They were now pitted against kings who were already supported by some sort of rudimentary national feeling; a feeling destined to grow in proportion as the political power of the Papacy declined.

This sense of nationalism, as might be expected, grew with the growing reality of national cohesion. At the great Universities, from the earliest stages

[1] See, for instance, L. Choupin, *La Valeur des Décisions,* etc., p. 12.

onwards, students were officially grouped under their different "nations". The Hundred Years' War between England and France was in some real sense a national war; and neither the universality of the Church, nor the universal use of Latin among educated people— factors which have often been credited with far more influence than they really exercised—did much more to end that national conflict than to kindle it. Definite appeal to French national feeling (that is, to such feeling among the barons, since citizens and populace counted for little as yet) was made in 1300 by Pierre Dubois, a pamphleteer, who supported Philip IV of France in his quarrel with Boniface VIII. Dubois starts from the postulate that "it is a peculiar merit of the French to have a surer judgment than other nations", therefore the peace of the world will best be assured by subjecting it to French rule. Popes, he claims, have in fact more often kindled than extinguished wars; let the Papacy barter its claims of world-sovereignty to the French king in exchange for an adequate pension in money, and world-peace may thus be secured. Here, of course, Nicholas I's violation of the Gelasian Concordat brings its revenge. For if, at one time, the Pope may overstep his appointed limits, and interfere with the rule of temporal princes, on the plea of pacification, then at another time the temporal ruler may find exactly the same excuse for infringing the Concordat in his own favour. Moreover, from about 1250 onwards the Papacy had become so much more definitely a political power, involved in all kinds of struggles for temporal sovereignty, and carrying these on by ordinary political and military methods, that this retort of Dubois was felt to be peculiarly effective. Marsilius of Padua, about the same time, based his anti-papal arguments to a great extent on the same ground, that the Popes had notoriously created more wars in Europe than they had prevented. Machiavelli, a few years before the Reformation broke out in England, referred to this again as a notorious fact—and, indeed, the events of these two centuries between him and Dubois had done still more to justify the accusation (*Discorsi sopra la Prima Deca di Tito Livio*). Marsilius, indeed, is so important that a few words must be devoted to him here. He studied and taught first at the University of his native Padua, where political discussion and even philosophical scepticism were more flourishing than in most parts of Europe; he adopted medicine as his profession, and at Paris became Rector—roughly, equivalent to the modern Vice-Chancellor—of the University. Here, in collaboration with a French colleague, he wrote his famous *Defensor Pacis* in 1325 or 1326. The book is startlingly modern in thought; it breaks away almost entirely from what we should otherwise recognise as the medieval tradition; it provides perhaps the clearest among many scattered indications that, beneath the apparent consensus of opinion on all main points, much revolt went on even among University teachers in their private talks with each other. Marsilius is one of the very few medieval writers who rises to anything like modern historical methods; he sees clearly how many respectable traditions are quite irreconcilable with unimpeachable documentary evidence. Though he, like all his contemporaries, ventured no hint as to the spuriousness of the Forged Decretals as a whole, yet he exposes the unauthenticity of one of the principal documents, the so-called *Epistle of Pope Clement to James the Brother of the Lord,* by subjecting it to straight-forward common-sense examination which, unfortunately, very few medieval thinkers ever dared to apply to their historical documents. For (he notes)[1]

in that part which is entitled *Concerning sacred vestments and vessels, to James the Lord's Brother,* and in that entitled *Of the Common Life of the Apostles,* it is written as though Clement were describing to James that which Christ wrought with His Apostles. Yet this would have been great ignorance on Clement's part—not to say, presumption—to communicate magisterially the things which he himself knew only by hearsay, to the man who had been present among the Apostles, who had been one of the Apostles, and who himself had seen Christ. For who could best instruct the disciples at Jerusalem concerning the life of Christ and His Apostles? Could any man doubt whether an Apostle could do this best, or a mere successor of the Apostles? On this account, these sections must be reckoned as apocryphal. And, even if we grant that they were written by Clement (as some men maintain, relying upon fabulous traditions; nay, exceeding so far as to say that Clement, being Bishop of Rome, was of greater authority than the Apostle James in the Church of God) we must naturally ask these men: Why are not Clement's *Epistles* inserted in the Canon of

[1] *Defensor,* ed. Previté-Orton, p. 434.

Holy Scripture, as James's is? But, as to the things which in these Epistles will be seen to contradict the judgment of Christ and His Apostles, we will treat of these when we deal with the quotations from Scripture whereon these men seem to rely.

He then deals with the New Testament texts, and shows that they contain no assertion in favour of the medieval Petrine claims, but rather, on the contrary, sometimes show us St Paul or St James acting the part which medieval theology claimed for St Peter alone. St Paul (he continues) was the first true founder of the local Church of Rome. General Councils of the whole Church were, originally, summoned and presided over not by Popes but by Emperors. What the Pope possesses now, in 1325, he has gained mainly by successive encroachments. First the original systems of popular election have been gradually superseded; endowments have grown disproportionately, with accompanying temptations to worldliness; the power of the Pope and of the priesthood in civil affairs is not only a trespass but a mischievous abuse. The highest authority in Christendom, under Christ, is the Bible; and the final court of appeal is a General Council, in which laymen as well as clergy ought to be represented, and which the Emperor alone has the right of convoking. The Pope is not even a necessity in Christendom; true, he fulfils certain duties which it would be difficult to arrange for in other ways; but there is no inherent impossibility in the idea of dispensing with him altogether. Nor are these revolutionary theories of Marsilius due merely to a desire of flattering the Emperor, whose side he had taken in the then quarrel between Empire and Papacy, and to whose protection he owed his life. On the contrary, he doubts not only whether a universal monarchy is desirable, but even whether a monarchy of any kind is superior to a republic; so that, when Henry VIII ordered the *Defensor* to be translated in order to strengthen his case against the Pope, the translator had to make large omissions in order to avoid offending the King.

It was a further shock to papal power when Clement V and his successors left Rome for Avignon (1305–1378); and a still greater when the Great Schism (1378–1418) rendered it almost impossible for some years to decide between rival popes. Here, while St Catherine of Siena was quite certain that the Italian was Christ's true vicar, St Vincent Ferrer not only decided for the Frenchman, but undertook to prove by irrefragable logic that all who held to the Italian must be damned, except in so far as some might be excused by invincible ignorance. Then the Council of Constance (1414–1418), by asserting the superiority of general councils to Popes, temporarily converted an absolutism of several centuries into a constitutional monarchy. But further democratic pressure at the Council of Basel (1431–1443) resulted in reaction, and the last years of the Middle Ages witnessed a growing autocracy in the ecclesiastical as in the civil sphere.

For society was as yet unripe for anything like modern democracy. At the very foundation of medi-

eval political thought lies the emphasis on unity,
yearned for all the more passionately because society
was in fact torn for many centuries by almost ceaseless
wars from without or from within. It was the anarchy
of the Dark Ages that had given strength to the feudal
ideal. And, for the same reasons which had told in
favour of the development from anarchy to feudalism,
men gradually welcomed the development of feudal
semi-collectivism into the full collectivism of more or
less absolute monarchy, both in Church and in State.
"Through all the work of medieval publicists there
runs a remarkably active drift towards monarchy",
says Gierke; "and here we see a sharp contrast between
antique and medieval thinking". As Professor H. W. C.
Davis has written, "good government in the Middle
Ages was only another name for a public-spirited
and powerful monarchy".

CHAPTER X

The Church and the Economic World

HITHERTO we have looked almost exclusively at the academic or official side of medieval thought. But we must not stop here; it is one of the most dangerous errors in historical perspective to judge an age by its greatest men only, though of course we must take the great men first. Historians have frequently exaggerated the efficacy of medieval discipline; and, in consequence, the homogeneity of medieval doctrine. We may see this in one of the most interesting of medieval doctrines, that of the just price in trade, with its corollary, the prohibition of usury.

Under that elaborate system of Civil Law which grew up and was systematised in the Roman Empire, the economic principle was that each man must look out for himself; the current proverb was *caveat emptor*: "Let the buyer be on his guard". But medieval Church law, and also the State, in so far as it allowed itself to be influenced by that law, tried to inculcate the gospel principle: "Do unto others as ye would they should do unto you". The earliest Christians of all were so far communists that among them there would be little or no trade. The Christian writers of the first four centuries were strictly Puritan in their attitude towards trade. A passage attributed to St Chrysostom, who died in A.D. 407, runs: "Whosoever buyeth a thing, not that he may sell it whole and unchanged, but that it may be a material for fashioning something, he is no merchant. But the man who buyeth it in order that he may gain by selling it again unchanged and as he bought it, that man is of the buyers and sellers who are cast forth from God's temple". In other words, you may buy raw material for your *work*; but to buy the finished article for *trade* is sinful, and only one degree better than usury. This, after all, follows logically from St Paul; if no Christian may go to law with his fellow-Christian, then there can be no extensive trade between Christian and Christian. It may be that these words are wrongly attributed to St Chrysostom, and are really by some later writer; but this would make them even more important from our point of view at this moment; for it would prove that this extreme prejudice against trade was current even later than the saint's death; moreover, the words were incorporated in the *Corpus Juris Canonici*, compiled in about 1150,[1] which enjoyed enormous authority all through the Middle Ages and beyond. This text, literally interpreted, was not only incompatible with trade on any great scale, but could scarcely be stretched even to make room for a village shopkeeper. The Church receded from this untenable position; but only gradually, and, for the most part, unofficially and even unconfessedly.

[1] Gratian, *Decretum,* Pars 1, dist. 88, cap. 11. See *History* for July 1921, p. 69.

Even in A.D. 1250, St Thomas Aquinas, a theologian conspicuous for his moderation, finds some difficulty in explaining St Chrysostom's words away, and regards commerce quite plainly as a thing rather ignoble in itself, as a product of fallen human nature; there would have been no trading in Paradise. St Antonino, writing a generation after Chaucer, is of the same opinion; he does not actually contradict St Chrysostom, but tries to soften his condemnation: trade is not a laudable thing in itself; but it may be laudable if the trader is content with making just an honest living wage for himself, and if, so far as his gains amount to anything more than this, he gives that superfluous income to the poor. Thus arose the characteristically medieval notion of the Just Price. A man has a right to moderate profit, enough to keep him and his family in the decent comfort natural to his station in life, whatever that may be, but he has no right to anything more.

With this we may all sympathise as a moral ideal; but there remains the extreme difficulty of translating it into practice. At bottom, it reduces economics to a matter of conscience. It starts from the principle that *good* or *bad* depends upon the trader's intentions. If he intends to serve the public, and to content himself with a moderate wage for his service, this is good. If, on the other hand, he intends to get more profit than that, his work is immoral. In certain comparatively simple cases, this medieval theory was capable of more or less successful enforcement in practice. National governments and local governments did already in those days what we ourselves did on so large a scale during the War, and have gone on doing to some extent even since the Armistice: they fixed prices not only for a good many of the necessaries of life, but also for wages. Bread, for instance, was to be sold by a sliding scale, according to the market price of corn at the moment. Beer, again, counted as a necessary; the price at one time was 1½d. a gallon for best, 1d. for moderate, and ½d. for small beer. This "Assize of Ale" did, no doubt, succeed in standardising the price to some extent, but far from completely. Practically every man or woman who brewed broke the assize, by selling their drink too weak or too dear; and the fines amounted, in practice, to the same as if the dealers had kept the law, but had had to buy a licence and pay duty on the drink, as they do nowadays.

With the rapid development of trade and commerce from about A.D. 1100 onwards, partly in consequence of the Crusades, modern problems began to come in, and especially the problem of usury, that is, of lending money at interest. Usury, as at first defined by churchmen and by lawyers, was a perfectly simple idea, capable of the clearest definition in a dozen words. To lend money, and to receive back one farthing more than the sum actually lent, was usury: and usury was a mortal sin, for it was explicitly forbidden in the Bible; and we have seen how to the medieval theologian, as to almost all theologians until comparatively modern times, there was no possibility of questioning anything that was clearly stated in the Bible. In 1150 the problem was really beginning to be serious, and rapidly it grew into a question of life and death for commerce. If men might not take interest for money lent, then evidently society could never outgrow the primitive village conditions. Real freedom of commerce necessarily meant freedom for interest; and that freedom was obtained not by facing the question directly, and proclaiming explicit alterations in the law, but, indirectly, by altering the original definition of usury. This development was strikingly similar to what is happening now in America with the Volstead Act. We are told that there is practically no chance of changing the American constitution again; alcoholic liquors will always be forbidden in words; but, on the other hand, a great many people seem to entertain strong hopes that the words of the law will be so interpreted by the executive authorities, in a good many States at any rate, as to open the door for a moderate sale of alcoholic liquors. If this parallel which I suggest between the conditions in Europe seven hundred years ago, and the most modern conditions in the most modern of all world states, seems to you at first sight too bold, let me ask you to follow in patience the facts I have now to put briefly before you. For those facts I have given full vouchers in the quarterly magazine called *History*, for July, 1921.

In the matter of usury, as in the matter of trade, the Church built everything upon the question of a man's intention. If you lent money in order to gain thereby, that was usury, and a mortal sin. If, on the other hand, your intention was to help your neighbour, and you took nothing but what might suffice to cover any loss which you might be put to in thus helping your neighbour, then there was no harm in taking interest. For example, if I have to borrow in order to find the money which I lend to my neighbour, it is natural that I should expect my neighbour to repay me that interest which I am paying to the third person; and, similarly, in all other cases where my kindness to my neighbour involves definite loss to myself, it is right that he should make it up to me. Even this, of course, was a relaxation of the original Christian prohibition; but it was a very natural relaxation. And though the Church allowed this compensation for actual loss incurred, it refused to allow any compensation for what was called the "cessation of profit". It never accepted the plea that I might justly receive compensation for the fact that whatever money I lent to my neighbour was rendered useless to me for the time being, whereas, if I had not lent it, I might have traded with it and increased my income. To have admitted this plea, according to the philosophy of that day, would have been to fly in the face of nature. For by lending my neighbour a cow, I do incur actual loss; if I lend her for a year I lose not only a year's milk, but perhaps a couple of calves also. But if I lend £100 I lose neither milk nor calves; gold and silver do not breed like animals; it is only Shylock, the usurer, who "takes a breed of barren metal". Therefore Church law expressly condemned all taking of interest in mere compensation for estimated loss of profit from the money thus lent; and we must remember that, on all these important points, the State accepted Church law, in theory at least. This distinction between the righteousness of compensation for actual loss and the wickedness of compensation for keeping barren metal idle is quite logical in theory, whether we agree with it or not; but in practice it turned out almost as difficult to work as did that other distinction between good and bad intentions.

Perhaps the first important set of cases to which the newer doctrines of usury had to be applied were cases of what we now call a sleeping partnership; the Middle Ages called it *Commenda*. A shipman or merchant, for instance, went on a long and expensive voyage; it was obviously to his advantage that some other man should help to swell his capital, and should receive a proportionate share of the profits, after wages and working expenses had been deducted. But, by such an arrangement as this, was not the lender taking usury? According to the earliest Church definitions, he most undoubtedly was; to accept anything beyond the sum actually lent had for centuries been condemned as a mortal sin. Even by the later and more indulgent interpretation, was he not clearly taking a breed of barren metal? For the lender of that £100 was sitting quietly at home; it was the shipman and his crew whose labours produced whatever was produced beyond the bare capital; what right had the idle lender to claim any share whatever in their labour?

That was the problem; and here, as so often in history, facts came in and forced the passage which theory was doing its best to barricade. For at least a couple of generations before the Norman Conquest, merchants in the Mediterranean ports, which were by far the most advanced in civilisation, had been practising this sleeping-partnership system, this *Commenda*. During the next two centuries it became so common that even Pope Innocent III, in A.D. 1206, advised that a wife's dowry should be invested in that way, as a sort of gilt-edged security. Yet, in a treatise of popular theology written just about that same time, we find that the moralist expressly pilloried the practice as notoriously sinful, and explained its prevalence by the fact that nowadays men, in this degenerate thirteenth century, will do anything for money, and will respect the successful moneymaker without considering the morality of his methods. In these circumstances, we need not be surprised that the problem was presently attacked directly by Pope Gregory IX, who dealt with the question in a decree which goes by the name of *Naviganti*. In that decree he puts the case of the lender who receives back, in addition to his principal, a share in the profits of the voyage, and decides bluntly, in two words, *usura est*: "That is usury". This was, in effect, nailing the old flag to the mast; Gregory thus upheld the Christian tradition of 1000 years in flat defiance of growing commerce; there must be no trade but such as a man can do in his own little boat, with his own little capital. From that point of view, the decree *Naviganti* is comparable to the Volstead Act in its uncompromising assertion of principle. We may be surprised at the boldness with which Gregory IX defied the whole world of great trade to which his master Innocent III, himself a great Canon Lawyer and a very courageous ruler, had paid silent homage. But a greater surprise lies behind. Gregory IX, the author of this sweeping prohibition, commissioned St Raymund of Peñaforte, a Spanish Dominican, to compile a fresh book of Papal decrees which should be supplementary to the first volume of Canon Law. Naturally, Raymund included Gregory's own decree *Naviganti* in that collection; the whole book then received formal Papal ratification, and the *Naviganti* decree thus became Statute Law for all Christendom. I believe that it was never formally abrogated until all the older collections were superseded by a new code of Canon Law in 1917, thirteen years ago. Those two fatal words, therefore, were still on the Statute: *Usura est.* Yet Raymund, writing a book of his own on Canon Law, a few years after he had put that decree upon the Statute Book, confessed that some theologians still decided flatly against the Pope's ruling. And, a few years later again, St Thomas Aquinas dealt with the question in a section of his great *Summa Theologiae*, which became the foundation of all Church teaching upon the subject of partnership, down to the present day. St Thomas decided that the lender's risk might truly count as labour on his part, and so he might avoid that impious attempt to breed from barren metal. If the lender draws up a contract compelling the shipman to refund the sum lent, whatever may be the result of his voyage, then (says St Thomas) he does commit usury; for he reaps interest without earning it. But if he shares with the shipman the chance of losing instead of gaining, then that risk may count to him for labour, and his investment is not usurious. It is a common-sense solution, worthy of so great a philosopher, and showing great boldness in its breach with earlier Church tradition. But there was the flatly contrary decision in Canon Law; and Canon Law, theoretically, was of such binding force that any man disputing it was a heretic.

In those circumstances, when St Thomas and the great philosophers after him were ignoring the Pope's plain words, it was natural that conservative churchmen on the one hand, and the civil authorities on the other, should sometimes ignore St Thomas. Thus, on the one hand, we find preachers, even down to the Reformation, still defining usury to their flocks in the old crude terms; anything that is accepted beyond the bare principal is usury. On the other, civil authorities abandoned altogether that question of good or bad intention, and all those refinements of scholastic logic, and attempted to settle by practice a difficulty which had led the theorists into such a labyrinth. The Kings of France, from at least about 1300 onwards, practically permitted all usury under royal licence and under certain conditions as to the rate of interest: other princes, even Popes, did the same.

The Middle Ages end, then, amid these divergencies

even in theory, and the still greater divergencies in practice. On the one hand, we must give the men credit for the courage of proclaiming a strict moral principle in the face of the mere indulgent "let things slide", "competition always brings things to the right level". For that courage, we must give the Church all credit; and we must blame the nineteenth century for having so far lost sight of that old ideal. On the other hand, the overstrictness of the medieval law brought contempt upon the law; boot-legging became a profitable trade. There is abundant evidence that usury increased rather than diminished during the latter part of our period. Benvenuto da Imola, the Bolognese Professor who, in Chaucer's day, wrote an elaborate commentary upon Dante, expresses naïvely what men were saying around him in busy commercial Italy. After describing the miserable figure cut by these sinners under the rain of fire to which Dante condemns them, he adds that, nowadays "he who taketh usury goeth to hell, and he who taketh it not tendeth to penury". Even St Francis's crusade against money-getting had not stemmed the tide. The Franciscan Nicole Bozou, writing just about a hundred years after St Francis's death, complained, "Nowadays, the old fashion is changed; for those who once avoided to give such men the kiss of peace in church, are now ready to kiss their feet...and they whose bodies were wont to be buried in the field or the garden are now entombed in churches before the High Altar".

CHAPTER XI

Popular Religion

THIS matter of Just Price and Usury was worth dwelling upon at some length, not only for its intrinsic interest, but also because that department of social life in the Middle Ages is only one of many in which we shall stray very far from historical truth if we imagine that the medieval hierarchy and the Universities, or even the whole body of clergy, can by themselves give us an adequate conception of the average man's ideas. For the average man, unconsciously yet very truly, was in effect dictating to his betters, even in regions where a superficial view regards him only as submitting to dictation. Many of the most influential medieval doctrines (as, for example, its lurid eschatology) had in fact grown up from below. The schoolmen did indeed defend these tenets with every reinforcement of logical subtlety, but with regard to the tenets themselves they had no original choice. With all St Thomas's originality in many directions, he was obliged in many others to start from premises inherited from past generations during which the hierarchy had gradually adopted and consecrated popular beliefs. The same is true even of some among the most important Church ceremonies and holy-days. Of all the saints in the Roman Calendar, probably 75 per cent. at least owe their position to popular choice, not only before Alexander III (d. 1181) reserved canonisation for Popes alone but before even the earlier stage at which the diocesan bishop had possessed similar powers. Again, what is now one of the most striking red-letter-days of the Roman Church, that of Corpus Christi, was due almost entirely to an enthusiastic girl and a young unlearned priest. Their suggestion was taken up by the then archdeacon of Liège, destined afterwards to become Urban IV. In 1246 the Bishop of Liège ordered the festival to be kept in his diocese; and in 1264 Urban, as Pope, published a bull in its favour. Yet even about 1300 the feast was not universally recognised; and it was Clement V (d. 1314) and John XXII (d. 1334) whose decrees did most to render it universal. But demand creates supply; simple minds demanded simple solutions of the most complex problems of life, and thus the official answers were dictated, to some real extent, by the intellectual limitations of the questioners. The lofty abstractions of Paulinism or of the Johannine writings could scarcely have worn through the Dark Ages without a heavy admixture of some such alloy. For unity's sake, Church teachers were compelled to be all things to all men, even at the expense of taking, here and there, a permanent tinge from that to which they had condescended. And this idea of unity outlasted the Dark Ages; it may even be said to have attained to its most definite expression only when these were past, and when the world had settled down into the comparative stability of the thirteenth century. By that time, two generations of great thinkers had toiled to weave the accepted beliefs of their day into one harmonious philosophic whole; and then came the temptation to stiffen in self-satisfied repose. A modern Scholastic can boast, with no more than pardonable exaggeration: "The thirteenth century believed that it had realised a state of stable equilibrium; and [men's] extraordinary optimism led them to believe that they had arrived at a state close to perfection".[1] In so far, therefore, as medieval thought can be described with any approach to truth in a single sentence, it may perhaps be characterised as a struggle for unity; a worship of unity which amounted almost to idolatry. We may apply to the Middle Ages that half-true epigram which reflects one side of the French Revolution: "Be my brother, or I kill thee!" With the same half-truth we may put into the mouth of a medieval thinker: "Be at unity with me, or be burned!" We ourselves are too ready, perhaps, to take divergencies for granted and even to make a merit of them. But the passion for outward unity was one of the main forces in medieval reconstruction; it was the most obvious rallying point in Church and State. The mystic has been admirably defined by Dr McTaggart as one who feels a greater unity in the universe than that which is recognised in ordinary experience, and who believes that he can become conscious of this unity in some more direct

[1] M. de Wulf, *Philosophy and Civilisation in the Middle Ages*, p. 208; cf. p. 18.

way than in that of ordinary discursive thought. It would seem, therefore, that all constructive ideas must have a strong element of mysticism; and this is one justification of the modern revived interest in the Middle Ages. We may hold that there is more real unity in modern society, beneath its outward divergencies; and yet we may feel that we have something real to learn from those who strove harder than we do for outward unity. At any rate, for them it was one of the necessities of their position; here, for many centuries, seemed the only escape from anarchy in State or in Church.

We have here only the specially strong and enduring manifestation of a phenomenon which is common elsewhere in history. Rightly enough, men will catch at any escape from anarchy. If the *ancien régime* lasted so long, it was because the only alternatives were the tyranny of a squirearchy, or else the helpless confusion of a populace which lacked both leaders and political experience. Napoleon, again, was rightly welcomed as the alternative to a mob-rule which had still so much political sense to learn before it could succeed. Just as the peasants of the Dark Ages were glad, on the whole, to rally round the nearest fighting man, and even commit their liberties to him, so they were quite content to rally round the priest. The Church, with very little question, with its strong sense of social solidarity, gave them neighbourly and religious warmth; her teaching and example, even when all necessary deductions have been made, were definitely on the side of brotherhood. It is true that her higher speculations were mostly above the head of the average man; but even here there was some real infiltration, and we find not infrequent examples of high mystical enthusiasm among the unlearned. Her ordinary ceremonies, and many of her beliefs, since they had sprung to so great an extent from the multitude, were therefore acceptable and comfortable to the multitude. It is noteworthy that, in the Dark Ages, heresy seems to have been always unpopular; heretics were often lynched, and sometimes, apparently, not even by priestly initiative. Anything rather than anarchy; and the average man, quite apart from his uncultured dislike of anything strange and perplexing, realised dimly that these dissentients were not strong enough, either numerically or individually, to rebuild Church or State if either were destroyed.

But civilisation advanced and knowledge increased; then the average man became more thoughtful, and therefore more critical of an institution which had not sufficient elasticity to keep pace with the general growth of society. One cause of strength in the Scholastic doctrine was that it often rested on foundations of popular belief; but, in its very completeness, in the perfection and calculated imperishability of its structure, it was apt to find itself finally in conflict with popular feeling, which, in its very nature, is changeable and slowly progressive. Nothing can be more dangerous than the belief that we have arrived at a state close to perfection. There is good common sense at the bottom of Lord Balfour's cynical answer to the friend who showed him the Woolworth Building in New York and extolled it at the same time as fireproof from top to bottom—"What a pity!" At all times, the severest test of a half-truth is that a philosopher should pursue it to its logical consequences. Given the premises which were accepted by hierarchy and laity alike, Aquinas was impeccably logical in proving that it is the Christian's duty to remove obstinate non-conformists at any cost, even at that of the stake. But to lynch in the heat of passion is one thing, to kill by implacable logic is another; and the Inquisition was never popular, even among men whose ancestors had with their own hands cast the heretic into an extemporised bonfire. Its unpopularity increased when it became evident how definitely it was nourished by the fines and confiscations imposed upon rich heretics; and, again, how fatally it lent itself (as in the cases of the Templars and Joan of Arc) to purely political purposes. Moreover, the most unimpeachably orthodox scholars sometimes recognised that one of the main tenets of the heretics, their objection to oaths, could scarcely be condemned in the face of Christ's plain words. Therefore the cruelties and injustices of the Inquisition—very great, even when we have stripped the story of all exaggerations—go far to account for such an utterance as we find recorded against a heretic of Toulouse in 1347: "This man Peter said also that, if he could hold that god who, of a thousand men whom he had made, saved one and damned all the rest, then he would tear and rend him with tooth and nail as a traitor, and would brand him as false and traitorous, and would spit in his face". The wave of popular mysticism which seems to have begun in Dominican circles on the upper Rhine at the end of the thirteenth century, and thence to have spread by the trade route to the lower Rhine and England, showed, among other manifestations, a strong tendency to escape from the cruel theology which, as very commonly preached and understood, is set forth without exaggeration in this man Peter's words. This humanitarian effort is noticeable in three of Chaucer's contemporaries, Rulman Merswin of Strassburg, Juliana the anchoress of Norwich, and the author (or authors) of *Piers Plowman*.

This last-mentioned poem serves better than any other medieval document as text for a disquisition on the mind of ordinary men in the later Middle Ages. Nobody, it is true, can understand medieval life who has not read Dante's *Divine Comedy*; but *Piers Plowman* is an even better index to the mind of the multitude. In that poem we have a picture of all classes, including the very poorest, as reflected in the daily thoughts of educated fourteenth-century Londoners at their best. The very incoherence of the book is in this sense one of its main merits; the author is always thinking aloud; he reveals all his moods, untroubled by fear of self-contradiction; he mirrors faithfully the medley of ordinary human thought. He shows us one charac-teristic which ran through the whole Middle Ages and survived, for instance, with so many other medieval factors, in societies like that of the *ancien régime*. This is the emphasis on privilege side by side with law, and, it may almost be said, on privilege even above law—an emphasis which is not really contradicted, but rather strengthened, by those who would remind us that medieval privileges were part of medieval law. Radical as the author is in politics and in religion, he accepts the distinction of classes as God-ordained. Not that the compartments are absolutely water-tight, but no interchange is contemplated under normal conditions; he looks upon it as a social scandal that bondmen's bairns should be made bishops and that soap-sellers or their sons should be knighted. As a matter of fact, very few such cases as the former are recorded in all the range of medieval history; hence, no doubt, the greater scandal to the average thinker. There was much else to exercise this fourteenth-century Londoner's mind. The Hundred Years' War and the Black Death, he sees, have shaken society to its foundations. At one extreme are ex-soldiers and labourers taking advantage of the plague to claim higher wages and idler days, though St Paul wrote, "he that will not work, neither shall he eat". At the other, we have a boy-king led by evil counsellors; a nobility and a squirearchy against whose oppressions Peace formally petitions to Parliament in the name of the poor; and Commons who would willingly seize the government into their own hands, if only they dared to bell the cat. With all this social disorder the author has little sympathy, though he is poor himself, living from hand to mouth, and men take him for a madman because he will not make obeisance to great folk in office or in silks and furs. One of his main themes is this of the dignity of honest poverty and work. Peter the Ploughman (he says) can lead us as straight to heaven as the parish priest himself; yet this, after all, must be by the old and narrow way: "they that have done good shall go into eternal life, and they that have done evil into everlasting fire". Meanwhile, it is a disjointed world through which we have to find our way from the cradle to the grave. Money rules everything; the man who can bribe is the man who grows to greatness; justice is bought and sold; the great town houses are built and inhabited by wholesale dealers in rotten stuff, who "poison privily and oft the poor people that parcelmeal buyen". Life is a jostle for worldly success; "the most part of this people that passeth on this earth, of other heaven than here hold they no tale".

Yet our author's own faith is unshaken; he steadily trusts the larger hope. Not that he sees his way everywhere so clearly; the whole book is full of theological problems which he attacks yet cannot solve. Nor can the parish priest solve them for him; the friar, again, for all his fat red face and bold verbosity, leaves him equally puzzled; and the professional pilgrim, when the real pinch comes, proves a broken reed. All of us, as loyal church-folk, wish to believe in papal indulgences; yet how can we reconcile these with the supreme value of good works? How can we reconcile predestination with free will? Why should posterity suffer for Adam's sin? Our poet himself grapples reverently with these problems, but he tells us of great folk at whose high table the after-dinner discussions are anything but reverent (B, x, 52):

At meat in their mirthës, when minstrels be still then tell they of the trinity a tale or twain, and bring forth a bold reason, and take Bernard to witness. Thus they drivel at their dais, the deity to know, And gnaw on God with the gorge, when their gut is full....

I have heard high men eating at table carping, as they clerkës were, of Christ and of His mights, And lay faults upon the Father that formëd us all....Why would our Saviour suffer such a worm in his bliss, That beguiled the woman, and the man after, Through which wiles and wordes they wenten to hell?...Why should we that now be, for the works of Adam Rot or suffer torment? reason would it never! Such motives they move, these masters in their glory, And maken men to misbelieve that muse much on their words.

But all these uncertainties, from which no thinking man can escape in any age, drive our poet more and more inward into the sanctuary of his own soul. For himself, he is sure of a few fundamental things. Truth is paramount, Truth is God Almighty. But Truth is not in mere intellectuality; to learn is "Do-Well"; to teach is "Do-Better"; "Do-Best" is to love. Heaven is not for the wise, as men count wisdom, but for the good. Solomon the wise is probably now in hell; yet many poor simple folk "pierce with a paternoster the palace of heaven". And, above all, when we have no other stay, let us contemplate the life and work of Christ. Christ died, Christ reigns, and we, if we fight the good fight, shall reign with him; that is the main theme for all the last cantos of this poem. Still, "fight" is the word. True, Christ is in heaven; true, again, that here on earth we have the Pope, Christ's vicar through Peter; but the history of the Church has been a sad story, for Satan had soon crept in after the Ascension, and had "coloured things so quaintly" that honest folk, ever since, have scarce known what to think. In this England of Chaucer's day the mass of Christians are described as a flock of shepherdless sheep; they "blustered forth as beasts over banks and hills, till late was and long". The professional pilgrim proved quite helpless when these folk, weary of the well-worn shrines, asked the way to a new saint, to Saint Truth; to that appeal he could only shake his head; that is a saint unknown to the Pilgrims' Way. And, now that Antichrist is preparing another and fiercer attack upon Christ's folk, who have entrenched themselves as best they can within the fold of Holy Church, it is the clergy themselves who become the worst traitors; first the priests, and then the friars. Then the enemy comes on more fiercely: where is Conscience, who has been set to keep the gate of Holy Church? "He lieth and dreameth", said Peace, "and so do many other; The Friar with his physic this folk hath enchanted, And plastered them so easily, they dread no sin".

Here, within seven lines of the end of the poem,

there seems no room for a hopeful conclusion. Yet the author's personal religion is proof against all shocks of disillusion and disappointment; he is "one of those rare thinkers who fight fiercely for moderate ideas, and employ all the resources of a fiery soul in support of common sense" (Jusserand). Christ reigns still; if His fold is thus taken by storm, then let us shake the dust of it from our feet and go forth as solitary pilgrims, "as wide as all the world lasteth", in search of the Christ that is to be:

"By Christ!" (quoth Conscience then) "I will become a
    pilgrim
And walken, as wide as all the worldë lasteth
To seek Piers the Plowman[1], that Pride may be destroyed,
And that friars may find their guerdon who flatter for gain
And counterplead me, Conscience. Now, Nature me
    avenge,
And send me good hap and heal, till I have Piers the
    Plowman!"
    And then he groaned after grace, and I gan awake.

The whole book, supported as it is by multitudinous indications from elsewhere, shows us the growth of a simple mystic religion among the people. And this, side by side with the well-known Renaissance of learning among scholars, nobles and merchants, with a general and growing impatience of moral abuses, and

[1] *I.e.*, Christ in the flesh. Piers Plowman, in this poem, undergoes the same sort of spiritual transformation as Dante's Beatrice. He begins as the peasant saint; gradually he becomes the type of humanity at its highest and best, the human nature of Jesus Christ. I have slightly modernised syntax and vocabulary in this passage, to avoid frequent explanations.

with concurrent economic causes, worked for the change from the medieval to the modern mind. Great churchmen, for generations past, had pointed out clearly that, unless means could be found for reforming the Church from top to bottom—*Reformation in Head and members* became the regular cry—from the Roman court down to the ordinary priest and his parishioners —then revolution could not be avoided. That revolution had been as long foreseen as the French Revolution of 1789; and at last the unavoidable thing came. Like all other revolutions, it brought havoc and unsettlement; but, for good and for evil, it made modern Europe. Intolerance was still the rule for many generations, and it may be argued with some appearance of truth that this intolerance was equally violent among all the contending parties; yet, in the long run, these party contentions have forced tolerance even upon the most unwilling minds. Facts have proved, what reason was proving only slowly and fitfully, that no party can have any hope of exterminating the other, and therefore that all must arrange themselves so as to live together in this world of bewilderingly various tastes and ideas. In this matter of toleration, one of the most important for human progress, the world has turned away, to all appearance for ever, from the mind that was natural to medieval Europe.